MW00778451

Originally From Dorchester

A Memoir

GERARD HEALY

The illustrations preceding chapters 4 (Lafield Street House) and 12 (Boys on a corner) are by Dennis Auth of Norfolk, VA. All other illustrations are by Luisa Rachbauer of Germany.

LifeRich Publishing is a registered trademark of The Reader's Digest Association, Inc.

LifeRich Publishing books may be ordered through booksellers or by contacting:

LifeRich Publishing
1663 Liberty Drive
Bloomington, IN 47403
www.liferichpublishing.com
1 (888) 238-8637

ISBN: 978-1-4897-0310-1 (sc)
ISBN: 978-1-4897-0311-8 (e)

Library of Congress Control Number: 2014916402

Printed in the United States of America.

LifeRich Publishing rev. date: 09/19/2014

CONTENTS

Dedication vii

Introduction ix

Prologue xi

Chapter 1   The Rat 1

Chapter 2   Being Schooled 9

Chapter 3   Ghost Stories 23

Chapter 4   Lafield 35

Chapter 5   Nothing for Nothing 47

Chapter 6   Fishflies 53

Chapter 7   Myths of Dorchester 67

Chapter 8   The Path of the Righteous 77

Chapter 9   Sky Pilot 89

Chapter 10   Trapped 103

Chapter 11   The Wall 111

Chapter 12   The Quiet Truth..121

Chapter 13   Gentle Fall..137

Epilogue..151

DEDICATION

To Sujin
and
The Lafield Boys

INTRODUCTION

This is a work of creative nonfiction. All events, people, and conversations depicted are real and true, although the precise words in dialogue and actual timing of the events may not be accurate. While I have consulted photographs, web pages, journals, and conducted conversations with others involved, my main source for the accounts that follow is my own memory. In the interest of privacy, however, some names have been changed.

PROLOGUE

The first time I heard the term, "Originally From Dorchester," I was at a meeting of the National Security Agency, or NSA. A retired Army lieutenant colonel and current government service employee, I was part of a team developing a battle plan. It was the type of mission one dreams about, working with an interesting mix of innovative planners from various fields – Infantry, Military Intelligence, Strategic Communications, and others. In the previous month, we received input from Central Command, Strategic Command, and numerous theater area experts.

In a way, I felt I had travelled far from my Dorchester days; but in the most important ways, not so far at all. The lessons I learned in that town had prepared me well for all that followed. My parents, teachers, kind neighbors, true friends, and the culture of Dorchester provided me with a solid base of values. Trial and error would continue fill in the gaps.

The morning had included healthy debates that ranged from what could be done to what shouldn't be done. Then, during the course of a short break, an Army major approached me. He'd recognized a familiar accent and asked if I was from Boston. "Yes," I responded, and from habit, added, "from Dorchester." A smile spread wide across his face and his eyes lit up. "OFD," he said. I looked back at him quizzically, having no idea what that meant. "Originally From Dorchester," he explained.

He told me how folks all around Boston had t-shirts, hats, and bumper stickers boasting OFD. His father was one of them. He'd grown up in the Fields Corner section of Dorchester, and had often told his son and his other children of the almost mythical place he called home.

Mostly with the courtesy of the Army, I'd already lived in eight states and even more cities by then. None of them came close to stirring the pride and passion of my own hometown. As the major spoke, I remembered and felt the same fondness for home his father had conveyed to him.

Years later, while writing this book, I became increasingly aware of how much Dorchester itself had influenced me, how I had absorbed as much of it, as it had me. The stories that follow are of the good, the bad, and beauty of life there in the mid-60s. I've never forgotten the town's lessons, and tried to never lose the spirit of adventure that it encouraged, even demanded. Like many others who've roamed far beyond its borders, I carry it with me always.

Events of 1964

1st appearance of Beatles on "Ed Sullivan Show"

1st government report warning by US Surgeon General reports that smoking may be hazardous

Roman Catholic Church in US replaces Latin with English

Cassius Clay joins the Nation of Islam and its leader Elijah Muhammad renames him Muhammad Ali

Rolling Stones' 1st tour as headline act

US female Figure Skating championship won by Peggy Fleming

"A Fistful of Dollars" with Clint Eastwood is released

US begins bombing North Vietnam

"Man from U.N.C.L.E" premieres on television

Dr. Martin Luther King Jr. announced as winner of the Nobel Peace Prize

Che Guevara speaks at the United Nations General Assembly in New York City

CHAPTER I

THE RAT

Dave and I had just left the corner, heading toward the schoolyard when we heard the noises. First, it was the bottles breaking, then curses, and then we saw the three boys outrunning the chasing mob. Both of us, 11-years-old, watched the older Wainwright Park kids chase down the Lucky Strikes (bowling alley) boys. We jumped up on the raised lawn of a corner yard.

Two very long lines of cars bordered Centre Ave. as it approached its collision point with Dorchester Ave. From the high ground, we looked over the cars and saw the three teenagers, all with the look of rats, running toward us. The slowest of them had a large head and a bulky build. The other two kept glancing at him, and he talked to them as he ran. All wore dungarees and white t-shirts. But the thick one in the middle also wore a black leather coat. My first thought was he was a true rat, wearing leather on a warm day like today. I figured the coat was likely what started the chase.

Back in the early 60s, the teenage world of Dorchester was broken into two camps – the colleesh and the rats. It would be many years before I figured out that colleesh was slang for "collegiate." I knew what rats were. Outside of Dorchester, they were called greasers. While the standard clothes for the colleesh included corduroy pants and button shirts, the rats wore black leather coats and carried knives, usually switchblades. They were trouble, and the leather told you that they wanted you to know it.

The two skinnier boys had outdistanced the kid in the leather, before slowing down slightly to let him catch up. Then the boy in leather tripped. It was the worst possible thing that could have happened, like blinking with a football just feet from your open hands and face.

If he kept his feet, the rat might have been hit by a few of the flying bottles, and the fastest runners may have gotten close enough to land a whack or two. But the three rats had a tough look, and the other kids weren't moving as fast as they might. They were bunched up, nobody getting too far from his buddies. But once that boy tripped, his world changed. Decades later, I still see it clearly – the rat going down.

"Shit," he said as his right leg went from under him. The three were about 40 feet ahead of the mob. The kid to his right grabbed him under his armpit, to keep him up. The other friend, slightly ahead to the left, glanced back at the crowd, at the kid who was helping, and slowed his pace. It was a brave choice.

"Go," said the one in the middle. He had not looked back, but could, no doubt, hear the running and yelling close behind him. I was stunned by the hesitation of his friends. The mob was at full speed: in seconds they would be caught. The rat in leather, being half-dragged now, pushed the boy on his right with his arm while the momentum of his own body brought him down. He yelled something else I couldn't hear above the shouts of the mob, and the two friends at last picked up their pace, as the one in leather hit the ground hard.

About six kids continued past the fallen rat, chasing his friends. The rat rolled, turned, and swung his arms out toward the first boys to come for him. Dave was already off the lawn. He ran to the space between two parked cars, crouched down, and watched intently.

Four boys were now struggling with the rat. Two were rolling on the tar with him, the others kicking at him. The rat struggled up and dove at the two who were kicking. One of them went down and the rat went through the opening, picking up speed. But the slow runners from the gang now caught up to the action. A boy in full stride hit the rat. He went down, harder this time.

I jumped from the lawn and ran toward a parked car in the direction of the downed kid. More of the slower runners had caught up. One of them pushed me aside and grabbed at a car antenna. He twisted it quickly side-to-side. It wasn't coming off easy; he'd yank at it and then twist some more. He was breathing heavily and sweating. Then everyone was grabbing antennas, twisting them back and forth. On their faces were wild expressions, each boy's skin tight with crazed looks that resembled fear. I wondered why they would be scared. The one in the leather coat had good reason: I could understand that. Yet somehow, his body movement relayed less fear than the others. He was contained, still in control.

Then, even some of the boys kicking the downed rat got the idea of the antennas. As they left to twist them off the cars, the rat saw his opening. He jumped into a half crouch and busted between two kids, running and stumbling through the t-intersection out into the middle of Dot Ave. Breaks squealed and drivers hit their horns, but he made it to the other side and headed toward his home turf. It was about a quarter-mile away, but it might as well have been on the other side of the world.

Some of the other boys who'd given up on catching the rat's friends were jogging back toward the crowd when they spotted the leather coat. They crossed the street, two of them taking him to the ground, and the hounds moved in for the kill. There were swishing sounds as the antennas cut the air and smacked off the leather coat. That must be why he kept it, I thought. I would have ditched it for speed during the run.

I understood now that this must be how murder happens. Like animals smelling blood, the fifteen or so Wainwright boys converged on the one. Some kicked; others tried to whack with antennas. It was the sound of small winds, Whoooo, Whooooo, Whoooooo, Smack, and Smack. I knew their thoughts. They wanted to have something to talk about later, something they did. I'd heard the bragging in the schoolyard before: I could hear what was coming.

"Did you see that? I kicked him right in the side." Yes, they would talk of their bravery. It was a time of happenings and they would not be caught on the sidelines.

"I could hear his ribs crack . . . Man!"

"My antenna caught him right on the cheek, cut him clean."

"You know he would of got away if I hadn't tackled him." On and on and on. Whooooooo. Whooooo. SMACK, SMACK, SMACK.

"Watch it," someone yelled; "look out," another. Some of the gang started pushing at others as antennas bounced off their arms. As they backed off, the rat, tired and bloody, saw his last chance. Somehow he got to his feet and broke through the crowd again. But he was much slower. There was blood on the side of his face and on the sleeve of his coat. He would be caught. He could hardly keep his feet moving: all his strength had been bled or beaten out of him. I wondered if he knew this would happen when he pushed his friends away.

Still, there was no sign of panic; he kept looking and moving. It was like he'd been through this before. I wondered if that was possible.

I watched how he moved and could feel his thoughts. He just had to keep moving, keep busting through. But I could see that his legs were giving out.

The crowd caught him again outside the Centre Lounge. The kicking was furious. All those who missed him before were now in on the action. For those doing the kicking, the danger had past; they fought, desperate for a piece of the bragging rights.

It was then I realized I was going to watch someone die. I looked for Dave; he'd crossed the street already and was crouched between two other parked cars.

"Da-ave," I yelled, voice shaking. "Let's go." I should do something, I thought. But, what could I do? I looked at the crazed gang. They were all much bigger. That boy had tossed me aside like I was nothing. We were 11; these kids were 16- and 17-year-olds, and they'd gone insane. It was too late. They would kill anyone who moved into that zone.

I looked over to the gas station. There was no attendant outside. The doors to his shop, always open, were closed. Normally, the street had shoppers coming up the road, old ladies with their wire carts full of brown grocery bags, heading toward Saint Mark Church. They would stop and talk to whoever they met, at least a hello, and if they knew the other person, a long conversation would follow. They talked of the weather, of their friends, of the prices at the store, of the Old Country, of the manners of kids today. But there was no one there, no one talking.

Under his dark hair, Dave's pale face looked back for only a second, his eyes wide. He wasn't going anywhere. I thought of running back to the corner – just leaving – but I was too ashamed. I knew I would stay: I had no choice. Something bad was going to happen and I was in its grip too. I ran to the parked car next to Dave, squatted, and finally looked again toward the beating.

Only the backs and the legs of the boys could be seen. They were kicking into the shadows at the entrance to the bar. The rat was hidden beyond them on the ground. I couldn't see him but I knew he must be curled up, just taking the hits. Then the door of the Centre Lounge burst open. A man took a quick look and then yelled back into the bar. Seconds later three big guys busted through the crowd.

"What the Forque!" an Irish brogue yelled, followed by, "You Forquers!" Then the big guys started pushing the kickers away, one of them taking a few swings. Two boys were still kicking at the kid, and one of the Wainwright boys pulled at his coat. I ran forward a few more cars just in time to see the rat, over on his back, kicking and holding tight to the leather as the old guys dragged him through the doors. He was hurting, but he was alive.

The last-minute escape seemed a miracle. Who would have figured three guys from the Centre would save him, especially with him being from Lucky Strikes, not even from the neighborhood? I reminded myself that the rats were the ones who always started the trouble. Who did he think he was wearing that coat into the neighborhood? I walked over to Dave.

"I thought they would kill him," I said.

"Yeah," Dave said slowly. "Me too."

The beating had been the most violent thing I'd ever seen; yet Dave's voice held disappointment, like he'd been cheated out of something.

I was glad the rat didn't die. He never gave the gang the pleasure of seeing him yell or cry, or even look scared. He wasn't about to quit or let them take anything from him. I'm pretty sure now that it was his fearlessness, more than anything else, that drove them into madness. I began to understand why his friends were so slow to leave him. And as much as I was shaken, I was glad I'd seen it, seen him. These lessons you didn't learn at school.

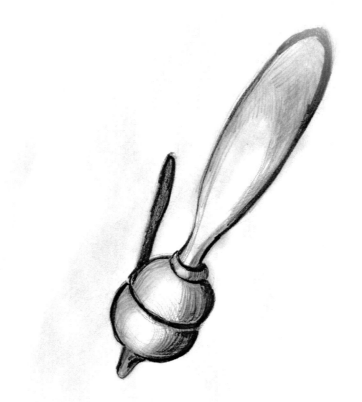

"The Clicker"

CHAPTER II

BEING SCHOOLED

Paul Jones was a bit of a troublemaker in school. Not that he would speak out loud in our fifth-grade class, or argue with teachers; the Notre Dame nuns who ran Saint Mark Elementary back in '62 put up with none of that. Nor was he one of those who started fights in the schoolyard.

Being of average height and weight, and unremarkable in about every way, Paul tried hard to go unnoticed, and did so well. His brown hair hung down to the middle of his forehead, and his face was of the fleshy type that bled easily, from even a scratch.

In the schoolyard he lingered behind as the rest of us boys raced to one end of the fenced-in yard. While we pushed each other, and argued whose turn it was to start the game of Bulldogs, he would stand off to the side kicking at a rock or just looking around the neighborhood.

What else he did early in the recess I can't say since getting Bulldogs started took some effort. We got only a half-hour of fresh air the whole day at school, and the time spent figuring out who was going to be the number one bulldog was a tiresome affair.

"I did it yesterday. No way I'm it today."

"But you did good, come on."

"No way."

"Come on."

Five minutes of this debate would drive some sane member of our lot to the breaking point. "All right. All right!" he'd surrender. "I'll do it."

Malley Hooker, a kid with a solid build, but not much speed, would occasionally be that kid. As the number one bulldog, he would jog out to the middle of the schoolyard, turn around, and face the 30 or 40 of us. On his command, the game began, Malley – the bulldog tagger – against us all. Our job was to run, dodge, and to streak across the schoolyard untagged.

Like a zombie's bite, Malley's touch immediately converted each touchee, past allegiances instantly forgotten as each tagged boy became another mindless bulldog in the middle trying to convert the untouched who dared to cross the yard. The last untagged boy – there were no girls – earned bragging rights, but continued to run until tagged.

At this point, Paul would have strolled over to a small group of girls. He avoided the groups with the tough ones, like Debbie Hanley. Paul had at least enough sense to stay away from her: instead, he'd stroll toward those with pretty dresses, those who jumped and giggled. While we plotted our routes and studied the orientation of Malley's body, Paul's eyes roamed elsewhere.

Naturally, I felt sorry for Paul. It was true, he probably would have been one of the first kids tagged and spent the rest of Bulldogs chasing the clumsiest of runners. But having to resort to hanging out with the girls; I mean – that was pretty humiliating. He did his best to look unbothered, and at that time, I believed he accepted his sorry fate with a resigned, monk-like dignity.

It was halfway through seventh grade when I first noticed a mysterious pattern emerge: more kids – some who were even fast runners – had joined Paul on the sidelines. Kids whom a year earlier had pushed him just for the pure fun of it were now buddying up to him. For some elusive reason, Paul was emerging as someone to know.

Always the neat dresser, after school Paul began wearing brightly colored shirts – actually drawing attention to himself. He didn't wear sneakers, but shoes that always looked new. And with his new friends, he was getting a little louder. He'd say things I couldn't understand, and add, "you know what I mean," and laugh. His walk changed too – like he had more energy; not enough to get him running across the schoolyard, but he moved less jerkily, and looked less jumpy.

One day, my best friend Kevin told me he'd seen Paul at Bradley's, the local store. Paul had been arguing with his mother – actually raising his voice to her. As surprising as this was, Kevin had more.

"You'll never guess what they were arguing about," he said.

My blank face looked back at him.

"Clothes," he said, dropping it like an anvil through water. He had a way of looking to the side, Kevin did, when he had drawn your entire attention to himself and just wanted to make you wait. "He was telling his mother what to buy."

"He was telling her?"

Kevin was grinning now. "And she was letting him."

Unbelievable.

To think such mothers existed. Fat chance that Kevin or I could've gotten away with any of that. More likely I'd have been thrashed to within that one inch of my life I'd so often been warned about.

These events that surrounded Paul were puzzling and unnerving. Now, I don't want to mislead. I hadn't noticed them all at once. I don't even remember thinking about them until that day in the classroom, or shortly thereafter. Weeks passed before I gathered my thoughts on Paul. Back in the schoolyard, there was only the feeling that something mysterious was going on; there were clues I didn't quite understand.

Sister Julia Cecelia, a squat nun who moved with quick, sure steps, was a clue. I noticed how she emerged more frequently from the schoolyard shadows during recess. She would head toward Paul and his associates as they talked with girls. The girls too, seemed to have changed; they strolled farther from one another, and more than giggled, they laughed loud. But as Sister moved toward them, the group would dissolve into pieces.

Of course, I caught only glimpses of this activity at recess. My main attention was on the game. I watched how short, but thick, Ronnie Mack was able to cross the lot not once, but twice, sometimes three times when he was the only runner left. Like the others, I marveled at how he, all alone, could out-run 40 game bulldogs. I studied him hard to learn his secret. Sure, he was fast, but no faster than two or three others of us. When I finally caught on to his trick, its simplicity was surprising.

Before he took off, Ronnie walked and jogged back and forth in the holding area. At first, I noticed only a few of the guys in the middle doing it. When Ronnie turned, they would drift in his direction. When he crossed onto the playing lot, I stayed back, watching. Whenever he approached a collision point, he slowed down, turned, and adjusted the pace, eyes reading the crowd. Closer to the mob, he broke to the right, 40 kids shifted to that side of the playing field, leaving the entire left half of the field open, and the kids kept banging into each other and bunching up as he maneuvered.

Now, everyone knew to change directions during a run. What I hadn't noticed before was how Ronnie was maneuvering parts of the group into each other. I'd thought he was being chased, but that wasn't it. He was maneuvering them to where he wanted them to go. He knew – as we all did – which runners were fastest. His moves drew the slow ones between him and the quick ones. He'd change direction until the setup was right, then he'd go for the opening. If the group had been looking in a mirror, they would have seen the mistakes -- surging forward too close together, getting bunched up, and working against themselves. Perhaps they would have spread out and held their own ground. But, of course, there was no mirror. They saw only Ronnie and nothing about what he was doing, or what he was making them do. They shifted mindlessly and bounced into each other. And there he was, making his moves, watching, adjusting his stride, then breaking free across that yard within no one's reach.

When the bell went off, we went back to school. Our mouths shut and our bodies sweating, we marched through darkened hallways. Nuns, armed with "clickers," kept watch. The small medieval-like tools, held in pale hands, protruded from long, dark sleeves. From the bottom of each clicker five inches of hard wood stayed level with the ground. The second matching stick of wood, its tip resting on the first, angled up over the fulcrum of a small wooden ball. On the stick's opposite end, a nun's thumb would press down, raising the bottom end of the stick into the air. The thumb would push with pressure since a tightly wrapped elastic band struggled to keep the opposite tip pressed against the bottom stick. With the release of the thumb, the tip would snap back onto the bottom hard wood with a distinctive and menacing *click*, a bolt-action sound that silenced all.

A click from somewhere behind would remind us not to look across the hall at someone in the line marching the other way. A smile, or a wave, to such a person, would prompt, another more threatening click. Talking to the person to your side was sure to lead to a burst of mad clicking from a series of the hooded figures. Sometimes a hand would reach out and yank the shoulder of a careless whisperer. A black caul would bend low, a voice hissing into the hooligan's ear.

At such times, I would think of home. But, I knew that any complaint of school or the nuns would be met with little sympathy there.

"That's really bad, ha?" Such was my mother's reaction to most dismal accounts. Over the years, I learned that no matter how bad – or good, for that matter – things were here, they were far worse or more charming in the old country.

"In Ireland's schools, they beat your back with sticks until they broke," she told me once.

"The backs?"

"No," she answered, checking my mouth for a hint of a smirk, "the sticks."

By the time I made it to the seventh grade, my mother had been in America ten years. At 43 her hair was still a light, honey brown. With nine children, she carried a body more sturdy than slim. Neither plain, nor pretty, she had the confidence of someone comfortable in her proud Irish skin. Always to the point, the tone of her voice told more than her words. The good of the old country came with a softness that could envelop a room. But its shortfalls were spoken with a harshness of stubborn resentment.

It was with harshness she spoke of Irish teachers.

She told me how they would go down the rows of students asking questions about to the previous night's lessons. The day I pushed her for more, she leaned back, gripping tightly the corners of a towel, before snapping it through the air and pressing the corners together.

"If the poor devil in front of you didn't know the answer, you were sent out with the master's knife to cut a switch," she explained. I watched as her eyes looked back some 30 years. The brogue in her words became more pronounced: the vowels in "the devil" switched to become "the divel" in her native tongue.

"And the poor divel who got it wrong," she added, "was beaten with that stick."

As she folded a few shirts, I watched myself eyeing grass for a stick out in the yard. And with a mother's instinct, she followed.

"And if the stick broke too readily, the fellow behind you was sent out to cut a stick for your own beating," she said. When I turned, she merely continued to fold the laundry.

"There are good sticks in Ireland," she said, as though remembering a few in particular. "Some of them pitiful creatures had to be sent home after a bloody beating."

So I marched along the dimly lit hallways of Saint Mark to another room. Through the door, we sat quickly in our assigned seats and faced forward. A turn to the rear was to risk the wrath of any teacher. But there were some brave lads emerging in the seventh grade, and when Paul turned completely around that day to only silence, we all breathed a sigh of relief.

At the time, if someone suggested I didn't like Paul, I would have denied it. I wasn't a friend of his, but held no grudges against him. After recess, I often noted how his clothes revealed no moisture. I figured he probably didn't like to sweat, and imagined he did little work at home. He had no brothers or sisters, so of course there would be no need for him to *keep an eye on them* or take them to the park, or even to go in the other room and tell them to shut up. I doubted that he had to run to the store to pick up the odd gallon of milk on any cold morning.

I figured Paul did pretty much next to nothing to earn those new clothes and shoes. But such a pitiful figure was he, even with his newfound fame, it was hard to muster any great feelings against him. His new friends, as my father might put it, were no bargain. They seemed friendly enough when the girls were around, but I sensed they would turn on him whenever it suited their interests. Paul, though, seemed free of such thoughts. With a newfound confidence in the classroom, he arose from his seat that day. In quick steps he crossed the room and checked the back door, making sure no adults were about. Then he moved to the blackboard and picked up a piece of chalk. A couple of his friends on the other side of the classroom were talking low to him. "Go on," muttered one. "Chicken," pressed another. He did as coached and started to write on the board: only as he wrote, his body blocked out his scribbling. I could only read it when he stepped aside.

"For a good time," it read, "call Debbie Lesley." Beside this was a telephone number. Paul's eyebrows were raised and the corners of his mouth stretched upward as he glanced toward his friends. It was an unnatural look, like a ventriloquist's doll with eyebrows and mouth strings entangled and stretched inside.

His friends laughed loud, and without a thought everybody turned toward the blonde girl with a normally pale complexion. But Debbie's face was now dark apple-red, and even Paul's friends' laughs stopped abruptly. The girl next to Debbie leaned over and talked low. By the way the friend moved her hands it was clear she was trying to make her feel better. For only a second the redness lightened before more waves of warmth rippled across the paleness.

Meanwhile, Paul, still at the blackboard wearing the bizarre smile, looked as though he'd told a joke he didn't quite understand; and now he wondered what it all meant. The rest of us just looked back and forth from Debbie to him.

After a few seconds, Paul turned back to the board and ran the eraser hurriedly, carelessly over his note. From above the board, he pulled down the map of the world and then strolled as casually as he could back to his seat.

Seconds later, Sister Julia Cecelia entered the room. No person was talking, no chairs squeaking, no desktops moving, no book pages fluttering, and everybody staring fiercely toward all areas of the room that didn't contain Debbie.

Sister surveyed the room with, it seemed, a psychic ability. She looked toward Debbie for a second or two, hesitated, and then swept the rest of the room with her eyes. When she walked to her desk, she did so slowly. Still in thought, she sat, and then quickly told us on what page to turn to in our books. When she began reading, Paul appeared to fold backward into his chair. Sitting several aisles behind him, I imagined he was smiling.

Sister Julius Cecelia, also known as Julius Caesar, expected everyone to obey the rules and took her job as an enforcer with a commander's sense of duty. On more than one occasion, it was she who yanked a hooligan from the line to issue a public scolding. And there had been that incident some years earlier with Ellen. Playing with a stapler, Ellen had somehow managed to staple the webbed area between her thumb and forefinger. She was one of the tougher girls, but gasped in her seat when it happened. I remember her, called to the front, hunched over as Sister Cecelia counseled her for not paying attention. It took about three minutes for Sister to peel back the ends of the bent staples with her fingernails.

"Quit your crying," she said a few times while picking at the metal tips. When she finally yanked the staple free, no comforting words followed; only, "now, take your seat."

Sister had mellowed not at all over the past few years. Paul knew that, we knew that, and I think that perhaps one blonde-haired little girl praying hard in her seat knew that.

A few minutes into the instruction, Sister abruptly rose from her desk and walked toward the blackboard. I'm fairly certain the entire class stopped breathing at that moment. At the board, she snatched up a piece of white chalk and turned to the class with enthusiasm. She was speaking words that were only noises in our minds: we were not listening, we were watching. Still facing us, her left hand groped for the dangling string that fell from the bottom of the map. Like an old window shade, after a quick jerk of that string, the map would slide upward, leaving an exposed chalkboard.

About 20 of us sat in the class; 40 eyes watched that hand reach for the string. Past the white thread it waved once as she still spoke, then twice. On the third pass the string met hand, and at precisely that second, Sister's psychic ability re-emerged. She gazed around the room, stopped speaking, and turned toward the map, giving it her full attention. Gently, she pulled the string downward, and then the whole world rolled up and away.

It should be noted that back in 1966, blackboards were still black. They were made of the same type of slate that skims nicely across beach waves. There is no denying the beauty of the slate's dark color and its smooth, shiny surface. But unlike the latter light-green models, the darkened slate required those writing on it to push hard, causing sharp white lines to be almost etched into its stubborn surface. And once carved into its surface, one could not easily erase the chalk from the stubborn models. It took sustained rubbing with foam erasers to turn the scribbled letters into a white wash of powdered chalk.

What Sister Cecelia saw on the board that faced her that day was not a professional erase job. No, it was the work of a lazy boy, and one who lacked the basic requirements of common sense. Beneath the thin film of pale powder, Paul's message could easily be read; and we all watched her read it.

When she finished, she turned smoothly and spoke only three words, each with increasing volume.

"Who," she said, pausing.

"Wrote," she added.

"THIS!"

Nineteen heads turned in unison to the front row, second seat from the left.

Only Paul's pathetic scull stared straight ahead.

"You!" she said, looking down, as if at the divel himself. "Come with me." Paul, in his fear and confusion, denied everything he had yet to be accused of. In barely contained rage she marched him straight out the door, and then closed it.

What happened exactly in that hallway became the subject of much debate for the remainder of the class year. There was clearly the sound of a scuffle – erratic bumps on the walls – then a loud thump, and a low tremor of vibration as the floor shook from a body collapsing onto it.

Sister's voice was calm, but loud when she returned.

"All of you. Out in the hallway."

In single file we moved. Outside, just beyond the door, Sister waited on our right; below her on the school linoleum, lay Paul.

"Look at him," she demanded, as I tried to hurry past. Curled up, face down, right arm over the side of his face. I couldn't understand why he didn't get up. We all walked past him about 30 feet, turned around, and passed him again as we re-entered the classroom.

In my seat I wondered what Debbie had done when she looked down at him; she probably wanted to kick him. But she couldn't have, not with Sister there. Though I didn't see them, so I don't really know,

I pictured his friends smirking as they strolled past. It seemed only natural that they would. They had talked him into it, made him do their bidding, and he had taken the bait and the beating, not them. They were clever: it was just the kind of thing to make them smile.

I spent the entire following year in the same class as Paul. He must have answered really tough questions, worn some outrageous clothes, or got into more trouble. No doubt, he did all that, but none of it survived the years. Always, his name brings back the sole image of the boy, broken and lying in the fetal position at Sister's feet.

He deserved it; I tried to tell myself back in the classroom. But I didn't believe it then, and can't now. I wondered how it might have been worse for him. *He could have been beaten bloody with a stick,* I hear my mother's voice say. But, of course, that's not worse at all. There's something noble about being beaten until the stick breaks: it's still you that walks away.

Although I'd like to believe it, I can never be sure that Paul's tragic moment occurred on the same day I learned Ronnie's great secret. The mind is funny like that, the way it weaves such memories together.

CHAPTER III

GHOST STORIES

In my earliest memory I stand shakily on two-year-old legs in a large room, wondering if I might stay up. Above, giants want me to do something, but what? The tallest of them, in dark clothes reaches toward me. I watch him, serious and still, and then he stands up straight, waving arms inward. My father, taller than the others, with the blackest possible hair and eyes to match, wanted me to come to him; even without any knowledge of words, I suspected as much. But as impatience spread across his pale face, I became certain those large hands were going to hurt me. My father, of course, meant me no harm; he only wanted me to walk to him. Behind me my mother and sisters, who'd come with me on the long plane ride from Ireland, made softer sounds.

When one giant bent low, his bright eyes sparkling, I knew he was nice and I steered toward him. Across the enormous room I stumbled twice, but managed to stay up, and when I got to Uncle Frank, other giants made happy noises and he held me steady, tenderly, for just a second. Then my father reached across and picked me up, and I erupted into tears.

Ever since that day Uncle Frank had a soft spot in his heart for me. But I had embarrassed my father in front of all who had come to the airport to greet us. After the long trip from Ireland, I chose his brother, not him, for the embracing welcome. In future years I would come to understand my father's proud nature, and realize how instinctively that innocent act would have hurt him. His family was important, and his disappointment was beyond any logic. It came from his heart – the place that mattered.

Denis Healy was born with the curse of asthma and a stubborn nature that would keep him in Ireland's heavy air and hey-strewn farmlands 40 years. For days at a time he's soak his bed sheets with sweat, struggling for the air to feed his lungs. It took a doctor's warning of death and my mother's earnest pleadings to finally uproot him and send him to "The States." The crippling effects of the disease, always hidden in shame from the neighbors, is what sent my father first, and the rest of us later, to Boston. It was that curse of asthma I would later credit for saving me from a lifetime of a bone-weary labor and the still-life boredom of farm living.

In his youth, Denis had traveled his homeland, working at odd jobs and practicing his skills as a tailor. But by the age of 20, the 40-plus acreage of farmland his mother left him in Glenfarne, County Leitrum, consumed most of his time and energy. He was 33 when he married an independent girl from the mountainous ridgeline across the Locoon Line valley. Then, seven years later he left the quiet life of the country village, and sailed across the expanse of the Atlantic Ocean, heading for Boston.

I was about eight when I listened to my father describe an early encounter in his new world. A friend met him at a train station and was leading him through town. Sitting stiffly in his chair, Dad's head tilted forward, eyes wide and voice hushed.

"Sure he turned right, left, around a corner, and then another," he said. "He continued to turn every which-way a man could, going up one street, and down another," he added, in a voice of desperation and a face of sheer confusion. Lifting his hands a foot from the table, he let them drop lifelessly back onto it. "Jesus Christ," he said slumping into the chair. "I thought to myself, I'll never find my way back. And I'll be lost forever in this town."

I remember Dad coming home from his first job, before leaving for the second. At dinner, he always sat down to an enormous plate of mashed potatoes. Along with roast beef, steak, or some other form of meat, the potatoes would be covered in gravy, and to the side, some element of green – string beans, peas, spinach, or Brussels sprouts. Only after dragging his fork across the scrapped-clean plate would he enjoy the single can of ale. Then my three older sisters and I would line up as he held a shovel-sized spoon of cod liver oil to our mouths. The fluid, threatening to escape over the sides, rocked slowly back and forth. In one hand we held paper napkins pressed tight beneath our chins as, one by one, he guided the spoon into our stretched-open mouths.

Afterwards we sometimes read to him from a schoolbook as he enjoyed his workday's 30 minutes of home life.

By any rational person's account, my father was a good man. He worked tirelessly to provide for his family at fulltime and part-time jobs each workday. He paid the bills, including the tuition for the Catholic school we attended. But the world he knew and the one I envisioned could not have been more at odds.

While he toiled at instilling some work ethic and practical knowledge into my stubborn head, I longed only for adventure. On weekends, trapped in the basement of our home, I held a light while the old man worked on teaching me the value of carpentry. Building a chair, or a workhorse, fixing a window frame, or sharpening a tool were some of the projects. Still and mute I'd stand, debilitated with boredom, trying to understand why anyone spent something as precious as time *working*.

Standing there, I'd picture friends tossing baseballs, climbing trees, or pitching pennies. If it was summer, I'd see them diving into refreshing beach water. At the end of the long extension chord, beneath the exposed bulb I held its thick, rubbery base. And more often than not, when he'd move, I was a step behind.

"By God, you can't even hold the light," he'd mutter sternly while, zombie-like, I'd shift position, casting the light over some penciled line he'd drawn so carefully across a ragged piece of wood.

Shortly before my seventh birthday, Dad paused the complaints about my ineptitude. He even stopped me in the hallway once to ask what I'd done that day at school. I wasn't sure of this new game. Then he started talking about a special present I might get for my birthday, pushing me to guess what I thought it might be. It wasn't new sneakers, and it wasn't a baseball glove, I learned quickly.

When the big day arrived, he waited till the cake was done and everyone had moved to another room. He watched me closely as he handed over the wrapped present, telling me to be careful to hold only the top of the strangely shaped object. Seconds later the flimsy paper lay shredded on the floor and I stood staring at my prize.

Stripped naked, a small saw gawked back at me with jagged metal teeth that stretched out from a child-sized red handle. I thought it a cruel joke at first, and looked up. In a glimpse I caught the hopeful expectation in his eyes before all sense of joy drained from his face.

Opening his hands wide, he breathed heavily and turned. All the preparation he had stored in the gesture – all his goodwill – spent on a losing venture.

I merely looked again at the saw. Did he really think I wanted something that would cause me to work? How often did he expect me to use it?

At six-foot, two, and skinny as a rail for most of his adult life, Dad's hair remained pitch black till he was in his sixties. Then within the course of two weeks, it turned all white. It did not grow in white: the whiteness began in the roots and proceeded to grow out to the tips of the thick carpet of hair. No doctor could ever say why.

On the odd occasion when Dad wasn't working, either at a job or at home, he would relax, sitting in a chair just thinking. But sometimes he could be coaxed into telling a story. It seemed at these times the ocean that separated us seemed to narrow.

Of all the stories, it was those of the ghosts I remember best. As he recounted the events, he seemed under some mystic spell, speaking much like a psychic medium with the memories escaping from him.

"Go ahead, Denis. Tell the story," my mother started in on him one night. Dad shook his then dark hair above the long face.

"Don't tell us you don't know how," my mother egged him along in a light, teasing tone. Two men were sitting at the kitchen table. Although both of their names are long forgotten, I remember one was a friend of my father's, the other, a stranger, though clearly a man from the old sod. On the sidelines I, and my three brothers, sat quietly. The setting for the story was a backcountry road of his hometown.

Before beginning, Dad looked directly into the eyes of the man he knew. It was the gaze of a man about to bestow a dear gift, searching his listener's eyes for evidence of understanding – to see if he knew the weight of it. Satisfied, he then glanced down to the table, clenched and unclenched his teeth and nodded.

"It happened by the old McMarrow site," he said. His friend asked a few questions, and Dad nodded again. "That's the one." Turning to the other man, he explained. "They found him dead in his bed – the old man," he informed him. "Some said he'd done it to himself." No further clues about the man or how he might have done "it" were offered.

Lifting his head Dad stared into the distant, dead air. Beyond the old McMarrow site, coming toward him walked a friend of his. Between Dad and that man was another, pushing a bicycle. He had his back to Dad, and was moving slowly about 50 yards away.

"It was dark, so I could only make out the shape of the man," Dad said in a mystified voice. "I didn't know him, and I thought to myself, *who could that be, on this road, out this late at night?*"

He was fairly certain he knew the fellow coming toward him. It appeared to be Mick John Frank, who would routinely travel the country road. But the fellow with the bicycle was a mystery.

"He wasn't riding the bike, just walking with it. Him – walking along the dirt of the road – and the bicycle on the grass beside him," Dad described. The rest of us listened, unmoving, as his voice went a notch lower. "And he had a lantern with a candle inside it, lighting the way." My brothers and I glanced at each other, trying to picture such a strange sight, while the men at the table smiled fondly.

"I thought, 'he's coming awful close to Mick John,' and neither one had waved or said anything," Dad continued. "Then, just at the last moment, without so much as a word, he stepped onto the grass and let Mick by."

Dad looked from one man to another to make sure they were following the story. I remember wondering at the shifting motions and growing interest of the men. I passed people all the time without saying a word. No one at the table was talking though, and I dared not interrupt. Dad's solemn expression kept all of us quiet. When the man continued around a bend in the road, Dad lost sight of him.

A moment later Mick John Frank approached Dad, who said his hello's and then asked his friend about the fellow pushing the bicycle.

"What fellow?" asked Mick John.

"The one with the bike, the one you passed."

"'What the hell are your talking about,' he told me'" said Dad. "And then when I asked again about the bike, he got mad."

"What kind of trick is this, Denis?" the man insisted with the voice of insult. "There was no man, and there was no bicycle!" At this point, Dad looked first to one of the men, and then to the other. They looked back, searching his face, perhaps wondering if there was more, or to spot the trace of a smile. There was none. "And when I got around the bend, there was no sight of the man," said Dad. "Nor his lantern."

The stranger at the table waited a few seconds before venturing his question.

"Are you telling us," he started in a careful voice, containing only curiosity. "That he was the dead man from the house?"

Dad looked back at him a few seconds and then deliberately shrugged his shoulders. "I'm not telling you that. I don't know who he was," he said. "I'm only telling you what I saw."

Mom was looking from Dad to the two men, as though still mystified by the story she'd heard before. Perhaps she'd waited to see if any of the details would change in this second, or third telling, if there would be a crack in Dad's demeanor, or if the men would scoff at the story.

"That's it," said Dad, looking up to Mom. "You wanted it told. It's been told."

The two men looked at my father again until they appeared sure there was no joke in it. After a few more gulps of tea, both men offered stories of Ireland's ghosts that they'd heard from others. Neither of them had ever seen a ghost for themselves, and it was only after a few more slices of Irish bread that Dad could be prodded into his second meeting with a ghost.

This one included Dad and a friend on a similar road, his friend seized by a ghost. Coming to the end of the story in the same trance-like manner, he suddenly banged down on the table with both fists, sending me almost bouncing out of my seat.

"In the name of God, be gone!" he yelled, in the voice of his friend who had shouted the words at the specter. With the rest of his body froze steady, Dad lifted his hands back up and spread them wide. "And as sure as I'm sitting here," he said in a voice barely above a whisper. "It disappeared." He looked around the table slowly and found only amazed eyes looking back.

My brothers and I knew better than to talk while the adults were speaking, so we said nothing about the stories at the time. Later, we helped clean the table and shortly after that were sent to bed. On the way toward the basement stairs, I remember committing Dad's words to memory.

"In the name of God," I recited. "Be gone." Even ghosts had a fear of God, it seemed.

With nine of us younger ones in the house now, my parents, three older sisters, Patricia and baby Desi, all slept on the first floor. In the basement room Dad built, Dennis and I slept in the big bed, me on the right, closest the wall, and Denis near the door. Opposite us in the two single beds Jacky lay on the left, Peter on the right.

It always seemed a little colder and darker in the basement, and that night was no different. An uncovered bulb by the stairway allowed only the small fading of light to seep into our room, where we quickly climbed into beds. It was impossible not to think of the stories as we lay in the twilight atmosphere. I believe it was Peter who finally spoke up.

"Do you believe it?"

Up until that night, we all would have laughed at the idea of spirits of the dead returning to haunt, or guide, the living. But if there was one thing we knew about our father, it was his insistence on honesty. He was nothing, if not a straightforward man. He told you what he thought in simple language and he never, in any of my recollections, told a lie.

"If anyone besides Dad had told it, I wouldn't," I finally answered.

"Yeah," someone chirped in. "Did you see his face?"

With about two years between each of us, I was the oldest at 13 and didn't want word to get around that I believed in interfering spirits. Brother Dennis echoed my thoughts on Dad. "Yeah, he was serious. And I know he wouldn't lie, especially to Ma or those guys," he said. "He must have seen those ghosts."

"Maybe they just have them in Ireland," offered Jacky. "You know it's really old over there." We all thought there might be something to that; maybe all the ghosts were in Ireland. After a few more considerations, we eventually tossed and turned ourselves to sleep.

About an hour later – maybe not even that long – my eyes snapped wide open. Something, and I'll never know what, had awakened me as quickly as though water had been tossed in my face. The hairs on my body stood straight out, and I was intensely aware of somebody, or some thing, near me. My whole body was flexed as I strained to hear a sound, some clue as to what had awakened me. Only the steady breathing of the others reached my ears. And then, a very warm hand fell onto my right thigh.

Racing wildly, my mind scrambled for the words.

"In the name of God," I said as forcefully as I could. "Be gone!"

Dennis shot straight up.

"What?" he said, his head turning from side to side. "What happened?"

The others followed. "What did you say? Jerry." It was Peter, who must have been only half asleep. "What did you say?"

In hyper-awareness I scanned the room, no one moving for the light switch on the opposite wall. Finally, convinced that the words had had their effect, I rubbed away at my right thigh.

"I'm telling you, a hot hand grabbed me right here on my leg," I said, rubbing the leg closest the wall. "And Denis was way over there," I added, pointing toward my wide-eyed brother. I was still making my case, when Dennis turned from me, to stare over at Peter.

Peter's eyebrows were stretched up high and he was pointing back toward the area next to Dennis. His hand was shaking and his mouth opened and closed twice, but no words came. Then Jacky straightened in his bed, the same fear on his face as Peter, eyes fixed on something. "The door," Jacky said. I looked toward Denis, and we both turned toward the door, but Dennis blocked my view and I couldn't see it.

"What is it," I yelled. And then I heard the door creak.

I doubt my heart ever beat faster, and in the next instant a burst of wild laughter came from behind the door. I immediately recognized the laugh as big sister Josie's. When she finally caught her breath, she stepped out from behind the door, yelled, "Boo!" and started laughing again.

From the kitchen, she'd heard my yell, and snuck downstairs in time to hear the story. That's when she got the idea of hiding behind the door and slowly opening and closing it.

After all that, it would be easy to say that Dad's ghosts were just stories, but to this day I remain convinced that every word he spoke that night was true. He could never have been that good an actor. His face, voice, and gestures all relayed fearful sincerity. There are ghosts, and of that he had no doubt.

The memories of Dad telling his stories are some of my fondest. Decades later, when I'd moved to the farm in Virginia, he'd already passed away. I've often wondered what he might say of my evolved appreciation of the land, the trees that surround it, and the creek beyond. If still alive, would he smile to know that my favorite tool – my prized possession – is now a saw? True, it's not one with a child's red handle, and runs with an engine, but it is a saw nonetheless.

On trips to Boston, I visit his gravesite. Rarely are people around the grassy area where he lays, and where I faithfully say the Ave he requested years before. It is a peaceful place with its nurtured grass and carefully placed flowers, an easy setting for smiling at once-abandoned memories.

Of course nobody believes in ghosts anymore, at least not in America. Maybe Jacky was right about that, all the ghosts being in Ireland. I can picture Dad back there, standing by a farm in the homeland that never left his heart, looking beyond the ocean. And he'd be smiling.

CHAPTER IV

LAFIELD

After living the first three years in the new country in the house of an aunt and uncle, the Healy's moved to Lafield Street. The home was a busy one. The neighbors in the other 14 three-deckers were stacked with adults and kids, many of them Irish. The new neighbors, friends from the old country, and relatives would often stop by. And when they did, Ma was always ready with her famous Irish bread, thick with the yellowed flour and raisins, waiting for butter and jam.

"Of course you'll have time for a cup of tea," was Ma's welcome refrain.

Often the neighbors' talk turned to the war in Indo-China, later called Viet Nam, or of the latest events in the Civil Rights movement.

For Ma, talk of war brought memories back from the time she spent in Belfast during WW II. She'd watched the American GI's ferried about on trains.

"All those boys – young, handsome men – laughing and joking; all about to be sent off to Europe and slaughtered on its beaches." She'd shake her head. "They knew it, and we knew it." It wasn't so much the war she opposed, only its terrible cost. When it came to Viet Nam, her opinion was one echoed by mothers across the country. "I just don't know why we're sending our own boys over there to be murdered."

Talk of the Civil Rights movement brought a hardness to Ma's voice: it was a topic where she held a personal grudge. She would speak of her father – "your grandfather" – she'd be sure to add, ensuring that I appreciated my own personal stake in the story. It was in the 20's when he arrived in New York to work with cousins in a New York speakeasy.

"There was no love for the Irish then," she told me. "'No Irish need apply' – those were the signs they'd hang in their stores." Whether or not such signs actually existed at the time is a matter of debate. But there is no doubt that is what my mother took from her father's accounts. "They treated us worse than their own dogs.

"First it was the Irish, then the I-talions, then the Jews. It don't matter. It's just the ones who got their money always trying to keep the new one's down. Don't you listen to any of that trash," she demanded. The idea that anyone would mistreat her own father left Ma with little room for debate. "You remember how your own people were treated. It's no different with what they're doing to the Negroes today." The word, "Negroes," a word of respect at the time, had yet to accrue its own baggage.

If one of my aunts were the visitor, the talk would turn to more pleasant topics, and usually to the old times. It was at that kitchen table where I first heard of the morning of my birth. My mother laughed every time she related the story of my sister Maureen's reaction. Sleepy-eyed, the two-year old walked into the room, looked me over, and asked proud Mom, "What cat had that?"

Apparently there was no shortage of cats and dogs, and new births on the farm. But the only dog whose name I can recall is Prince. He was a small dog, mostly black, but with some white around the neck. As I crawled or stumbled about, he was my constant companion, I heard, patiently watching me.

In Glenfarne, cars were a rare sight and drivers had no traffic to be concerned about. But one morning after I'd slipped out the back door and crawled around to the front, a car came barreling down the grass and dirt road. Before anyone could answer mother's panicked, "Where's the baby," Prince had already charged up the road and took the force of the car's onslaught, bringing it to a stop.

As visitors sipped tea and reached for yet another slice of Irish bread, I sat quietly, munching on my own thick-yellowed mixture with its brown topping. Stories of the homeland unraveled; stories of the best working horse in all Glenfarne – one by the name of Tom; the beautiful thatched roof grandfather put on the new home with the American money; and those ghosts that roomed the dark roads at night. If someone had an unusual dream, I'd listen intently as it was described in detail and Ma and her guest would explore it for hidden clues.

"We Irish put great store in dreams," Ma would explain later. "They tell us things we don't know about ourselves, and sometimes," she'd stress, "they tell the future."

Down the hallway and outside the front door of 10 Lafield Street was the most natural of all amusement parks – one run by kids. The noises of boys arguing and girls singing jump-rope rhymes rose above the occasional sirens and car horns.

It was a time when television sets were mostly black and white, and the channel choices were not hundreds, but only three. VHS tapes and DVDs were nonexistent. Computers were something only large companies had. Cell phones and I-pads were yet to be conceived and most houses had no air conditioning. The result of this was: if you weren't into tic-tac-toe or checkers, you went outside to play. And no one was driven to other neighborhoods; you made friends outside the door.

To us kids, parked cars that jammed both sides of the street served only as boundaries for many of our games. For whiffle ball, two selected car bumpers were first and third base, while stomped-flat brown bags or milk cartons in the middle of the street served as second, and home plate.

The telephone pole was the base of operations for hide and seek, or "Billy Billy Buck Buck." In the first game, someone leaned a head onto the back of a hand, resting on the pole as he or she counted, and others scurried under front yard bushes or inside tin trash cans that saved parking spots. In Billy Billy Buck Buck, some stout soul stood with his back against the pole, while another buried a head into his gut, and two more bent over behind the one below, creating a row of backs for someone else to jump on. The opposing team did the jumping, trying to break through to the ground. That failing, the jumper guessed an answer to the pole man's chant, "Billy Billy Buck Buck, Billy Billy Buck Buck, how many fingers do I have up?" A wrong guess and the jumper joined the row of horses, waiting for someone to try and break his back.

No tools and few rules were the guiding principles of most games, and Red Rover, Red Rover filled those guidelines well. One row of opponents held hands in a line chanting, "Red Rover, Red Rover, send Johnnie (or Kevin, or Jerry, etc.) right over." And Johnnie would come charging into the clasped hands attempting to break through. If he succeeded, his team got to clasp the hands, and if he failed, he joined the line he could not break.

Standing in the street, five feet from a curb, future gamblers tossed pennies, each trying to get his penny closest to the curb; collecting all those that fell shorter.

The sidewalks, with ridged boundary lines that appeared drawn in the cement by someone's pointer finger, offered continuous sets of squares. Opponents would stand on the outside lines of two boxes and place a discarded bottle cap on the centerline. A large ball was tossed with an aim to hit that bottle cap and cement sidewalk at the precise angle to drive the cap skidding across the opponent's line. The good part of a Saturday morning could be spent trying to get a ragged-edged Coca Cola cap over that winning line.

When there weren't enough kids to start a game, the Dolan's house offered the luxury of a garage. Climbing it and jumping into the pile of leaves or the snow humps, depending on the season, was a good way to pass time.

Sturdy trees in the neighborhood also kept boredom at bay and allowed for the age-old competition of "who can climb the highest?" Just over the fence in Kevin Dillane's yard was the tallest of climbable trees. Before the wind started blowing its slim trunk around in small circles and turning a climber's stomach to Jell-O, a young Tarzan could spot what was on the third deck of Kevin's back porch (usually a ball, a bucket, or some piece of clothing).

The girls on the street hopped on alternating legs between the chalked outlines of hopscotch, or played some version of jump rope. In a normal game, two girls would swing the rope and a third would hop over and duck under it. An advanced jumper would do the same in "pepper" as the swingers swung the rope at full speed; others attempted Double Dutch, where two ropes whirred in opposite directions, each slapping angrily at the tarred surface. In the tamer version of the game, the girls would sing rhymes passed down from earlier generations of jump ropers.

One day I watched two old women on the sidewalk just outside my house. One of them pointed to seven-year-old sister Maureen as she skipped along in the slower, normal version of the game.

"Did you ever hear such a thing?" asked the older lady in a black hat with a netted lace drooped halfway down her face. Her friend, who looked close enough in height and weight to be a twin, just shrugged.

"Sing that again," instructed the eldest.

Without missing a beat, Maureen repeated the jump-roping chant that had probably been invented by some World War II GI.

"Ohhhh, the girls in France, they don't wear no underpants," she recited, in the rhythm of the rope smacking the ground. "And the way they shake, it's enough to kill a snake."

The elder of the two turned back to her friend, raised eyebrows behind the thin veil.

"Do you know what you're singing about, child," she asked. Maureen only crinkled her face at the absurd question. How could she not know what she sang about when she just sang it twice?

What we didn't play in the street or the sidewalk we played in Kevin's back yard, the largest of the neighborhood. In the day, we'd adjust the rules of baseball to allow for playing with a large ball and disregard the requirement to run straight to the bases. At night, chestnuts shaken loose from the tree near his house, served as missiles we'd hurl at unthreatened acrobatic squirrels or squeaking bats.

But of all the games played out before Lafield's three-deckers, or in their backyards, the street's pastime was – with no serious contender – halfball. Even with the Internet I have been unable to track down with complete certainty the game's origin. There is no mention of any museum, or even a statue, to commemorate the innovator who devised it; no records indicate where the first game may have been played (though Savannah, Georgia is listed as a possibility), and to date no hall of fame exists to document the sport's most talented heroes.

Halfball incorporated all the requirements of a challenging city sport: speed, agility, hand-eye coordination, and split-second judgment.

It allowed for a variety of form, technique, and tactics: and not to be under-appreciated, the tools of the sport were easily and cheaply acquired.

Unlike hockey, with its skates, sticks, pucks, and – oh by the way – a hockey rink or frozen pond, halfball was the essence of Spartan efficiency. The equipment included a sawed-off handle of a discarded broom, and only half a ball. If used halfballs were unavailable, the event began with the search for a pimple ball. Many of the one-time popular balls, pierced by a sharp rock or just dead from age, had managed to find their way beneath the street floating on a surface of dank and smelly sewer water. A long arm and straightened-out clothes hanger with the hooked end intact could rescue such deadened balls through the iron gates above them. Then, with a one-sided razor blade, the operation to revive the ball was performed. A steady hand and sharp razor was requisite since a jagged knife's rough-cut would adversely affect the sailing ability of the two remaining halfballs.

The game's arena included two opposing sidewalks, the street between them, and one side of a three-decker house. A three-decker with tar or rubbery shingles was preferred since the hard-plastic coverings could shatter with the impact of a well-hit halfball. Of course, any unoccupied house, or one where the occupants were not home helped to ensure a game being played to completion.

Long before the Frisbee, some innovator had studied and learned the art of using the halfball's curved surface to coast over a city street toward a waiting batter. A good pitcher knew exactly how to grip the halfball, how to use arm motion and wrist snap to make the object almost unhittable, curving it in or away from the batter or sending it surging upward from the ground.

A clear contender for any future halfball hall of fame for the mid-20th century would be Jimmy Dooley. With his flowing left arm movements during windup he could distract his man at the bat, all the while adjusting the hold of the halfball in his right hand. Sweeping his arm low and dipping the fingers of his throwing hand, the halfball would often soar directly toward impact into the middle of the street; where, like magic, the ground rush of air beneath it would send the half-sphere rising back up, flashing its yellowed underbelly toward the batter, and accelerating in speed, Behind the plate, a catcher would stretch for the required catch. A swing and a miss mattered not if the catcher failed to grab hold of the halfball.

Jimmie's older brother, Mickey, was best known for his hitting ability. At bat in full concentration, he would miss nothing – the area the pitcher eyed, how much of the halfball's yellow tint was visible, the dipping shoulder. He would remember the path of previous pitches and wait for the break in the ball's path. A good hit by Mickey would send the rubbery sides of the halfball flopping end over end above the two or three fielders in the street until it slammed into the second deck of the outfield house for a triple, or soared up and over its roof for a home run – a truly impressive feat since the width of the street left such little angle of trajectory for the halfball's climb. The third deck also sufficed for a home run, but Mickey, as all of us, preferred the rooftop.

Often, crouched behind the batter was catcher, Mike Breen. Taller than most, Mike was an able journeyman at the position. It's likely that if any halfball rulebook is, or was, ever printed, it might not even mention the most crucial aspect of a good catcher. As every Little League survivor knows, it is to distract and annoy each batter with constant chattering.

"Here it comes. Here it comes. The high-riser. Get ready batter. Get ready. Get ready. Swing. SWING, batter-batter-batter," was one of the routines. And if there was a hit and a caught ball, Mike was ready. "What a catch, batter. You were robbed. What a crime! What a crime!"

A swing and a miss brought only sympathy from the man behind the plate. "Ohhh, ain't that a shame. What a swing!" And then, as almost an afterthought, "How'd that get by ya?" And although every good catch might carry its own reward, Mike usually highlighted it with equal energy. "Just call me Elmer, batter, like the glue, batter. Get it? Just like the glue!" A hop to the side, and Mike would send the halfball soaring back to the pitcher, a gleeful smile on his face. Undeniably, anyone who could catch a tipped halfball, on an upward spinning path deserved all the glorification he could heap upon himself. And Mike was up to it.

While the games and sports may have been the heart of Lafield, the street also had its House of Horrors element. Fear could sweep through the street with the suddenness of a thunderstorm, and two words provided all the thunderclap needed: *"Johnnie" and "Ramzee,"* the full name of the one sure to bring down the darkness.

From about first to third grade Ramzee would terrorize us Lafield Streeters in hit and run fashion. With a round face and a thick, rank body that resembled a beach ball stretched from top to bottom, he was a smaller version of our local butcher. Short, dark hair, fine as porcupine quills, reached out from the orb that was his head. Bigger, heavier and two years older than the rest of us, he would punch, push over, and kick anyone his thick legs could catch. Cats, dangling from hangman ropes, screeched in his backyard as he shot flaming arrows toward them. Then he would come for us.

Brian Jones was his victim one cold, wintry day. The patched-red cheekbones of Brian contrasted with the tight, white skin surrounding them. In his bare right hand he clutched two gloves he had just yanked off. Around his throat, one of Ramzee's gloved hands pinned him against his own three-decker.

"Take them," Brian squealed in terror. "Take my sled. Here! Here's my gloves. Don't kill me. Please."

Ramzee's face was one of surprise, but he continued to hold Brian against the wall. Sure, he figured he'd scare Brian, maybe even rub his face in the snow for fun, I suspected. But did Brian really think he was going to kill him? The very thought seemed to fill Ramzee with delicious joy, his eyes widened a bit, and a smile snaked up the sides of his mouth.

"Why shouldn't I kill you," he said, and hesitated. "I already got gloves." His body was stiff as he leaned forward, the outstretched arm bent slightly. "Give me money," he pressed. Brian's arms and legs stopped struggling. His mouth opened as though he wanted to argue, but no words came. Hands scrambled to his pockets and he squeaked, "Here, here. It's all I got. I'll get more. Just don't kill me."

Ramzee let Brian's fear fill him, as possibilities grew within that porcupine head. Then, from three-stories up, on his porch across the street, came the voice of Mr. Shaw. The Shaw's corner house faced Dix Street, allowing anyone on the back porch a full view of the happenings on Lafield.

"Hey! What's going on down there," Mr. Shaw yelled, looking over his bannister. Ramzee looked into Brian's eyes a few seconds more before releasing his grip. "Nothing. Nothing's going on," he yelled back, having already grabbed Brian's change. "Remember what you said," he warned, before running up the street. "About the rest."

The storm over, the wind subsided and the sun floated out from behind dark clouds. That's how the street was: a great place to be, as long as you kept your eyes open and had some friends and kind neighbors willing to do the same.

CHAPTER V

NOTHING FOR NOTHING

Cakes and pies filled the shelves inside the white van. Chocolate, strawberry, cherry and pure white frosting smiled outward. Mike and Jimmie, eyes wide on their own treats, stepped down the two stairs behind me and out into the sunlight. Of course I knew it was wrong to steal, but the crumbly brown crust and marshmallow-white whip cream pushed that thought clear out of my mind.

Johnnie, Paul, Kevin, and I headed up Centre Street in a slow jog, our arms around the stolen goods. Turning left at Althea Street, we went up a couple of houses before running through someone's back yard. From atop a chain link fence, I handed my pie to Jimmie, and then hoisted myself up onto the garage roof.

Coming to a peak, the roof slanted away into four quadrants. I slid my way to the quadrant furthest from Centre Street. I figured if the driver noticed anything wrong, he might run into the backyard of the house where he had parked, looking for the thieves. Sliding down to the lower rows of shingles, the downward slope protected me from anyone looking from three of the four directions.

When I stuck my head up and looked over at Paul, his wide face was already splashed red and white from the strawberries and cream. He'd dug into the cake with both hands and was licking the whip cream from his fingers. Long, dark hair hung over the food and hands. He appeared as a Viking who'd just butchered a poor animal and had no patience for cooking.

The six of us had spread out on the garage roof by now, but most of us were still just looking at the tasty treats sitting on our laps. Mine looked way too nice a creation to even consider disturbing – especially without a fork or spoon. I wondered how the pie top could have been made so smooth, and I studied the slightly dark brown crust with its flakey ridges.

Someone mentioned that the guy who owned the delivery van probably had a schedule to keep and wouldn't have time to come looking for us. That made sense to me, and I scooted up the garage roof a bit. Kevin and Archie, after complaining about the lack of forks, had begun digging into their cakes, too. Archie, the shortest and clumsiest of us, was using his hand as a knife in a karate manner. He pushed four fingers straight down near the middle of his cake, rolled the bottom of his hand toward the outside, and then scrapped his fingertips to the outside of the cake holder. When he got to the end, he cut another path at an angle from the first. It looked better than Paul's technique, but in the end he had to slide his fingers under the mess, and what came up was a ball of cake and frosting. Kevin poked a chocolate cake in the middle with two fingers and dragged the fingers to the edge, then dropping the peeled mess into his other hand. This gave him enough to drop in his mouth without smearing it all over his face.

I decided on Kevin's technique, and had just dragged my first two fingers of whip cream, cherries and crust to the edge when I heard Mike Breen's little sister, yelling. Pausing about five seconds in between yells, she called his name in the same loud, even tone four times. Then she said something that stopped all hands from moving treats to mouths.

"Mike, I know you can hear me. Mom wants you right now. And you're going to get it," her voice boomed. "You might as well come out right now."

Up till then, Mike had ignored the calls, digging away at his own pie, but with the threat, his long brown freckled face dropped forward. When he picked it up, he shrugged. "I got to go."

"Don't say nothing, Mike . . . Just stay here, she'll give up . . . Nothing about the cakes, Mike. Nothing." I immediately regretted my two-finger poke.

"Shit," Jimmie said. "Shit." He didn't have to say why. He lived on the third floor of Mike's house, and there wasn't anything Mike's Mom knew that Jimmie's Mom wouldn't find out about quick enough. He started pushing things around the top of his cake like he was trying to put it back together.

There was no possibility of fixing my once-perfect pie, so after a few seconds I stuffed the cherried mess into my mouth. It tasted great. By the time Mike came back, I was thoroughly enjoying my fourth scoop.

"Come on, guys," said Mike. Like a whipped middleweight, just trying to stay on his feet, his slumped body and guilty face told us we needed to know, everything except for the most important thing. Did he give up our names?

"I'm telling you they know all about it," he said, not really answering our questions. "Think about it. Who else hangs around here? What other group of kids could have done it?"

"Who exactly knows?" I asked, the realization that it didn't matter already sinking in.

Mike looked over at Jimmie. "Your Mom and mine, and your Mom wants to see all of us right now." Jimmie didn't look surprised at all, and we all started climbing off the roof.

"Bring the cakes," Mike said. "Mrs. Dooley wants to see them."

A great gang of thieves, I remember thinking. Why didn't Mike bother telling us how obvious it was before we walked into the van? Bring the cakes? Bad enough we were going to face the judge, but having to take the evidence to convict us along seemed an unfair, extra kick in the side.

Mrs. Dooley was about five foot, one, and maybe 100 pounds. When she smiled, she appeared the kindest person in the world. Like horses, mute and long-faced, looking down into a trough, we lined up before her front porch. From three steps up, she looked down at the miserable lot of us. Her face appeared a lot narrower than I'd remembered it and her eyes, like lasers, scanned our faces.

"Jerry Healy," she said with a world of disappointment in her voice. "You too?" The heavy weight of the cherries squeezed around the whip cream in my stomach, and I thought I would be sick.

"Feel proud of yourselves, do you?" she started. She nodded her head, as though agreeing with her own words. "Do you know that guy got up at 5 o'clock this morning to get those cakes and pies ready?" She glared out at us. "This isn't his only job, you know." Again, she waited for a reaction. Then louder, "Look at me!" With every pause now, she stared into each of our faces and eyes. "He works all week," she said. "Then gets up a 5 o'clock on his Saturday, and works until night."

I glanced around quickly, everyone else looking only at Mrs. Dooley. My eyes fell toward the ground, before I snapped my head back up.

"You think he does that for you to eat his cakes? Do you?" I'm certain none of us ever thought too much about the absent driver of the white van before facing Mrs. Dooley that bright day. And now, with our heads buried under a full trough of guilt, we were getting a clear view of our victim. "Or do you think maybe he does it to feed his wife and four kids?" Again, the look. "I hope you all feel proud."

One by one, we put the stolen goods up on the porch. I had about 75 cents, and I handed that over to Mike. Everyone gave him what he had in his pockets. I think the most came from Archie – about two dollars. We learned later how Mrs. Dooley and Mike's mother made up the difference, paying the driver when he came back later that day.

A few agonizing weeks after the heist we realized that our crime was so great that Mrs. Dooley decided not to tell our mothers, as was the custom. Maybe that's why I prefer to remember her with that welcoming smile and kind eyes.

I never heard the term "Neighborhood Watch" in all my years in Dorchester. But, without meetings or schedules, those parents had a system the FBI could only envy. And boy, could they lay the guilt on.

CHAPTER VI

FISHFLIES

B y the time we reached the seventh grade, the Lafield Street boys were seeking adventure beyond the neighborhood. In the summer of '66 we experienced one memorable trip 60 miles south to the shores of Horse Neck Beach. The Catholic holiday, The Ascension, had sprung us loose from school.

While Catholics across the world observed the miracle of Jesus Christ's body floating upward to heaven, Kevin, Ned, and I had thumbed our way to Fall River to ride the more powerful waves.

When it came to seeking adventure, thumbing offered a world of possibilities. Off Horse Neck's shores sat "Shanty's By the Sea." And behind that wooden shack, surfboards – hot wax melting off their backs – waited for us. Five dollars would get each of us a board for the whole day. Sure, the water would be "like ten ice cubes," as my mother would say, but that's how Massachusetts's water always felt. Less protected than Dorchester's Malibu and Tenean beaches, Horse Neck's water rose to six-foot crests, and could tumble your body around like clothes in a mad dryer. Its undertow was just as dangerous. Standing ankle deep, the pull sent your heels skidding along the sand like a skier toward the open sea. But if you want to learn to surf, you needed the power of those waves and you can't wait for really hot days and warm water. You go when you can, explained Ned. And he was right about that.

Out by the side of the road, intently communicating with every approaching car, Ned leaned over his thumb. *You can do it, slow down, nice and easy.* Veteran hikers, we'd positioned ourselves next to two vacant parking spots, on the far side of an adjoining street. Ned, leaning slightly forward, spoke lowly. "Here you go, look at this nice clean parking space, just waiting. This spot was *made* for you." A couple of inches taller than both Kevin and I, with wide shoulders, Ned had a swimmers build. He also had the confidence of a skilled high diver. Kevin and I listened to his words while studying the approaching vehicles, scanning each windshield for a clue to its owner's level of humanity. A rigid, straightforward stare from inside told us all we needed before the next car rushed by. "Where are you going, you fools?" Ned would scold. "Come back!"

A public school kid, Ned had snuck out of his house the night before with his bathing suit wrapped in a towel. Both were stashed under the bushes at the edge of his front lawn. The next morning, after picking up his lunch, he strolled out, absent all suspicious items.

For public schoolers, playing hooky (pronounced hook-ee) worked best on Catholic holidays. With the nuns' school kids swarming the holiday streets, the public schoolers slipped unnoticed into the stream. That didn't mean the police were no problem at all, though. They'd still pick up young hitchhikers, out of just plain meanness.

"Do you really believe it, that he just started floating up?" Kevin asked by the curb.

"Sure," I answered. "Why not?"

It was true; I'd never seen anything like that happen in my neighborhood – someone floating up toward the sun. As a matter of record, I hadn't seen one miracle – not food falling from the sky, not anyone walking on water. Yet I believed in miracles, or more likely, just wasn't quite ready for eternal damnation.

"A lot of people believe it, not just me. Why would they make it up?"

"Well," Kevin began, and I could see that he'd given it some thought. "If he was going to do it, why not when there was a huge crowd around, like up on the mountains when he was teaching?" Kevin had held this ace card till I committed, and I wondered briefly where he'd gotten this idea.

"More people would have seen it. He'd have got a lot more people believing and talking," he pressed.

Although I saw his point, I wasn't about to squander *my* soul. Eventually I reasoned that it probably wasn't his call. The older God – his father – probably told him his time on earth was done, so up he went. Kevin figured that as a pretty lame answer, but instead of arguing about it, we started giving Ned a hard time about not getting us a ride, and how little chance he had to win the "Golden Thumb." A combination of the quickest and longest rides was the likeliest way to earn that unofficial award, and all bragging rights with it.

"Five more minutes," promised Ned, before flipping his dark hair back out of the way. "A bunch of surfer girls will pull over right here, and take us all the way to Shanty's." This would trump all other considerations, a slam-dunk for bragging rights.

"Yeah," said Kevin.

"Sure," I said.

We'd all heard the Beach Boys singing about waxing up their surfboards and eyeing California girls, and those songs had captured every 1966 teenage boy's dream world. The previous summer, they'd sent us, and our towels, headed south for the first time. Catching about four rides, we'd swarmed onto Horse Neck's shores in three hours. In its water, we mostly clung to the boards that had tossed us off, and shivered uncontrollably on the shoreline before thumbing our way back. The girls had never showed, but the thrill of skimming across the water was great, each two or three seconds of it.

Later, we talked of the surfing and the different rides, the waves, the cars, and the characters we met along the way. Some drivers had said hardly anything, just wanted the company. Others told wild stories about how they used to thumb when younger. They'd had all kinds of adventures, gone all the way to Oklahoma or Florida, or met girls. Not ugly ones, either.

Those stories had a familiar, though never boring, ring to them. The girls were real polite at first, then asked the hiker if he was thirsty, and, no problem, here's a beer, and want another? The teller of the tale usually added, "yeah, that was something else, know what I mean?" We tried.

Other drivers would be into history or science, tell you the rocks from the quarries – right outside the window there – were used to build the Bunker Hill Monument, or how black holes in the sky sucked everything into them and held on, didn't even let light back out. On every hike to Fall River, we got at least one ride with a weird character or an unusual occurrence. And, if we weren't catching rides, we were talking about something else that happened before, something amazing.

When Ned's thumbing enthusiasm ran out, Kevin jumped up announcing that he was feeling lucky. We all knew the direct correlation between feeling lucky and actually getting a ride: it was a necessary ingredient. He tucked his pullover deep into his shorts and dragged three fingers across his brown hair. "Watch and learn." About my size at 5'5" Kevin wasn't as skinny as me, but not fat either.

On the curb, I shared my ongoing thoughts on miracles with Ned. Centuries ago, I figured, something unusual happened. Then, like our own stories, each time it got told, it got a little better. Add a couple of hundred years and those things evolved into flat-out miracles.

But, more importantly, I realized that the whole question of miracles came down to one thing: do you believe, or don't you? For me, the answer was a no-brainer. You believe it, nothing bad happened. You don't believe it, and are dumb enough to say so, you got trouble – trouble with the nuns, the priests, your parents. Then many years later, you pass away, and find out you were wrong, and there's Saint Peter with his clipboard and pen. He looks at you with that kindly smile and asks, "So, you want to know what hell looks like?"

Of course, I didn't understand how miracles happened. But there were lots of things I didn't understand. More importantly, the sun was shining brightly on my curb that morning, a day clearly warm enough for swimming. And we were headed for Shanty's, even if we weren't getting there anytime fast.

After awhile, we decided to head out for the expressway, taking turns thumbing along the way. Passing Hemingway Park, a group of kids played softball, no one was hanging by the entrance protecting the turf. Going through Neponset, we watched some old guy made his way into Looney Liquors. It was where 16-year-olds would get the local bums to buy booze for them. We passed the Eire Pub, where presidential candidates Reagan and Clinton would later drink beer (on separate occasions), then a McDonalds and its sign that bragged of a couple of million hamburgers sold.

Atop the expressway's on-ramp, two other kids stood, one with his thumb out, the other, in a white t-shirt, against the guardrail. The thumber cuffed a cigarette in his left hand, and every time there was a break in the traffic he'd raise it up quick and take a drag. Glancing back toward the cars, he'd turn to his right and exhale the smoke slowly.

Both had the confident look of Town Fielders, but up on the expressway the separate turf concerns didn't matter. We just nodded at each other and exchanged "hey's" as we went by. It was nice like that when you were on the road.

We checked out the cars as they came toward us, guessing which ones might stop. It was never a Cadillac or Chevy Cobra. A good bet was a car about five or six years old – Fords and certain Chevys were good, Volkswagens, too.

Ned was talking about someone who had thumbed down a bus once when Kevin's "Yeah!" alerted us to our first ride – a light blue Chevrolet. As Ned and I pushed off the guardrail, we spotted Kevin's grin. In the front seat two girls bounced to music.

Kevin held the door open, giving him time to clear the grin from his face. Slightly tanned skin and a friendly "hi guys" welcomed us in.

The driver, with a white blouse, was beautiful in the way only older women could be. The one in shotgun was pretty, but a bit shorter and slimmer than the driver.

"Where you guys going?" the girl in shotgun asked. As she did, the driver reached down, and "Hang On Sloopy" slipped away. The shotgun girl wore a dark blue pullover with a heart-shaped locket hanging from a gold chain. The heart was just a curvy frame, nothing in the middle so you could see right through to the pullover. The thin chain swung whenever she turned.

"Fall River," answered Ned.

"You're kidding. Really?"

She studied Ned's face to see if he was serious, and then pointed out that Fall River was a long way from Dorchester. When she asked how old he was, 13-year-old Ned hesitated only a second.

"Sixteen," he said.

Maybe it was the look on my face, or Kevin's, but they both laughed.

"Sure you are," the driver said, glancing in the mirror. "How about 13?"

"He's 15," Kevin lied, and added, "How old are you?" The driver glanced in the mirror.

"My, aren't you the brave one." Her voice had almost a musical quality. "Not afraid to talk at all?"

Kevin said nothing more.

Then she lifted her eyebrows up and down real quick, like, *I didn't mean anything*, and answered. "We're 17." Her friend glanced backward.

"You go to college," I asked.

"Not this year, but next."

"How about you, how old?" the friend asked. When she twisted, the locket clung tight to the pullover.

"Same as him, 15," I lied. And there I was, having a real conversation.

"We're all 15," said Kevin.

"You know, you guys ought to be careful about hitch-hiking. Do your parents know about it?" she asked Kevin. "It can be dangerous."

It was as if the front seat of the car kept going but the back had careened off the road. We could feel each other's groans, as our beach girls morphed into big sisters. Finally, Kevin answered. "Yeah, my mother says I should do it more often." We all needed the laugh.

When the driver turned the radio back up, "*We gotta get out of this place*," came through the static. The girl in shotgun kept twisting at the knob. It didn't help, but they were enjoying it fully, anyway. "*If it's the last thing we ever do.*" Their shoulders moved rhythmically. When it came to the chorus, they turned to each other. "Girl, there's a be-e-ter Life - for - Me - and - You."

It was pretty nice, just sitting there, watching them. When the song ended, one of them flipped through other stations while I quietly wondered if I'd ever go to college.

A few minutes later the driver pulled over by an exit in Milton, and we climbed out. After waving at the car, I turned to Ned.

"Sixteen?" I said, "Nice try."

"Your parents know where you are?" he imitated, in a voice nowhere as soft as the girl's. It was almost noon by then, and we still had a long way to go. That's when Ned reminded us that he had to be home by 4:30. Kevin and I had forgotten all about him needing to check in at home after school.

We figured out the rest of the day while we walked past the off ramp. We'd be to Shanty's by 1:30, surf till three, and with everyone then out of work, we'd get quick rides back, and there would be Ned – safe, sliding into home at 4:30.

About an hour and a half later, we got our second ride.

A creepy bald headed guy was driving. He kept telling us we should all know better than to be taking chances thumbing. "God knows who might pick you up . . . Crazy people all over this world," he warned. He was short, a little on the plump side and coughed a lot when he wasn't talking. Since I got the ride, I was in front.

About ten miles down the road, the guy pulled out a map.

"Hey, I can't balance this," he said, talking about driving and trying to maneuver the map, so he spread it across my lap.

I didn't say anything, just held the map.

"OK, we're here," he said, pointing with his finger at some spot on the map. I didn't even look at the point because I was thinking about how he was pushing down on that map way too hard. When he looked back out the windshield, his hand rolled over, the back of it heavy on my left leg. It was as if the hand was no longer attached to his arm; it just lay there like a fish, dead on its back, instead of rising up to the steering column where it belonged.

Still looking down, I noticed how quiet Kevin and Ned were in the back.

When I looked back at the guy, he just stared straight ahead. He didn't turn, didn't say "What?" didn't do anything but look out the window with that dead fish lying on my leg. When I pulled my left leg in closer, the hand flopped onto the car seat. After a few seconds, it came to life and went to the steering wheel. I was watching his face the whole time, but he made like he was real concerned with the traffic outside. No one was talking in the back seat. After we drove some more, the man reached down and ran his fingers across the map like he was looking for some road.

I pushed the map to the left and slid toward the window. When his hand came up, I folded the map and laid it on the seat between us. I didn't think about it; it was as though my hands had made the decision. Closer to the window, I rolled the handle a couple of turns and the air felt good.

It wasn't too much longer when the guy told us he was getting off at the next exit.

"You should have asked him if he was queer," said Ned. "I would have."

"He would have thrown us out right away," Kevin said, defending me. By then, we were only half way to Shanty's. When Kevin finally raised the question about turning back, I shrugged. Ned went through the time checks again, decided he could tell his parents that there was some problem with a bus, and he got kept in detention for being late.

That, he figured, would buy him another hour and a half. So, we decided to keep going and see where we were in an hour.

Two hours later we were headed back toward Dorchester. Two older teenagers, who looked like hippies – long hair and sleepy – gave us the ride going back before they dropped us off close to some town. Instead of continuing on, we headed toward the town so that Ned could make a call home.

By the time we got to the outskirts of town, it was starting to get dark. We'd already shared Ned's lunch, but were still hungry and everyone was quieter. As we walked, I kept feeling bugs bouncing off me.

"What the hell are these things?" Kevin finally asked. Ned stopped thumbing for a minute, bent over and lifted something off the ground. "Holy shit," he said, staring at the thing between his fingers. "These things look like fish."

Kevin pointed into the street. "Look in front of that car's headlights."

Dark objects, illuminated by the lights, were falling like a heavy rain.

"That's not rain. It's these bugs," said Kevin. He was now shaking his head and dusting some of the bugs off his shirt. They were all over the place.

I reached down and picked one of the bugs from my shoulder. It looked like an inch-long minnow. As it squirmed, I studied the transparent wings on each side of it. The body looked too heavy for the slight wings that were supposed to let it fly.

"I never heard of fish with wings," I said. "And I thought they needed water to breathe."

Kevin just shrugged, and then separated his towel from his bathing suit. He draped the towel over his head, tucking the suit under an arm. I followed his lead to keep the bugs from getting caught in my hair. Ahead, we were getting closer to the lights of the town. Ned, who complained that we looked like Egyptians, was still thumbing, and asked who was going to give a ride to a bunch of Egyptians? It wasn't long, though, till he gave up thumbing and put a towel over his head too.

We walked passed the town's one-story houses until we found a bar. Kevin stayed outside while Ned and I went in. From the pool table, someone lifted up one of the bugs and tossed it to the floor. At the same time, three people yelled, "close that door!" I turned and saw the fish bugs bouncing in off the ground, and did as they asked.

On the telephone, Ned had come up with a new story. He sincerely thought he had told his mother earlier about going somewhere after school. Someone named Billy, somebody's brother, gave him a ride there, and now the guy's car was having problems. I heard the voice on the other end of the line get loud and Ned stood up straight.

"She's pissed," was all he said after hanging up.

Out of other options, I called sister Josie and explained our situation. Much to my amazement, she didn't yell. She didn't threaten to tell Ma and Dad. She only interrupted me to find out what exit we got off the highway. Then she told me to get back there and she'd come for us.

Outside, Kevin had gotten the lowdown on the bugs.

"They call them fishflies and they flood this town about every eight years," he explained. By now, they were all over the glass window of the bar we exited. You couldn't even read the name of the place.

"Do they call them locusts?" I asked.

"No," said Kevin: he'd already asked some guy the same question.

The three of us put our towels back over our heads and headed toward the expressway. It was an odd sight, three Egyptians walking through the town, and the bugs all around. As we walked, I began thinking that maybe I had whole miracle idea upside down. I wouldn't have believed it if someone else had told me about it – flying fish that swarmed a town every eight years or so, falling from the heavens. And here we were, acting like it was as natural as rain.

Closer to the expressway, the bugs started to let up and we took the towels from our heads. Getting a ride wasn't so important now. With no sermon at all, Josie was on her way. I remembered how she'd laughed, thought I was putting her on.

"No way," she'd said. "Fish don't fly."

Songs of 1967

Ode to Billy Joe (Bobby Gentry)

All You Need Is Love (The Beatles)

Light My Fire (The Doors)

I'm a Believer (The Monkees)

Respect (Aretha Franklin)

Can't Take My Eyes Off You (Frankie Valli)

Ruby Tuesday (Rolling Stones)

Green, Green Grass of Home (Tom Jones)

Brown Eyed Girl (Van Morrison)

The Beat Goes On (Sonny and Cher)

CHAPTER VII

MYTHS OF DORCHESTER

There's a reason for the intensity in the eyes of those who watch a tightrope walker inch toward Niagara Falls, and it's deeper than any fear of seeing a man die. It's more intimate: it's because we have felt what he feels – the stretched, hollow belly, the sense of dread holding us back, and the adrenaline-powered joy pulling us toward our own edge.

Such a balance of fear and expectancy hung about me in'67. I'd survived the last year of elementary school with the nuns and would be attending a high school well beyond the neighborhood next semester. For the Lafield Street boys, it was a time before summer jobs intruded on our lives, razors scraped our faces, money became important, and before the mystery of girls enveloped each of us. We had just recently made the move to Wainwright Park, and were learning about the kids there, and more about the town.

One of the hangouts we would travel to was a pebbled strip of land, known simply as "The Tranie." It was a secluded stretch of land where darkness and beer, like trusted conspirators, mingled with the 14- and 15-year old taletellers. There, my strongest memories of Dorchester – those I never personally witnessed – were implanted. Entranced, we younger kids captured every nuance of the town's unofficial history, colored with some of its more notable characters, from the older kids.

The Tranie, short for The (Massachusetts Bay) *Transit* (Authority), was the perfect setting for such tales. Not far from the park, it was slightly raised from the earth and grass around it. Its wide, straight path was a secluded overhead section of Boston's Red Line. Thirty feet below screeching, bumping trains carried passengers from Shawmut to Ashmont Station. Above ground, the north and south borders of the Tranie were fenced off, isolated from its street borders of Welles Ave. and Centre Ave. The sides of the Tranie were lined with rugged trees and thick bushes. Beyond them, a string of backyards and then the backs of the houses that faced, like distracted parents, the other way.

The vegetation between the backyards provided useful concealment for any underage drinker who might dash toward a backyard. On the rare occasions when Boston's Finest ventured into the Tranie, they found no one. From the confines of the Tranie I saw the images of the giants who carved their names into a town with outrageous acts of bravery or stupidity: the difference never important. Mostly, the stories were true; at least I believed them to be so then, and still believe strongly in their essence.

Since my new comrades hung out at Wainwright Park, I heard often of its most fabled character. His name was Larry Harland, but to everyone, he was known simply, as "Head." Head was so named because of the large, almost square, noggin nestled on his shoulders. I'd seen him only once when I was about 13; he was quiet with assured confidence. When I turned too quickly at the mention of his name, he glanced back with a look of resignation. *Yes, I am that guy.*

One never got all of Head's exploits at once. Like a good drug, the dosage needed to be measured. I first heard of him in an episode that occurred when he was just 17. The story was, by no means, his most infamous, but captured best the essence of all the others.

It began at Head's apartment, a brick tenement that bordered the basketball court of Wainwright. Head lived there with a slew of brothers and sisters, but I never heard mention of either parent. The back section of his apartment held a porch that stood about 10 feet in from the park, and, importantly, about 25 feet up from the ground. From the street level, the surface of the basketball court dropped another five feet, leaving a 30-foot drop to the court. An iron rod, strung along tall poles surrounding the court, had at one time held wire mesh that kept basketballs from flying into the street. Over time, that mesh had worn away and only the rusty iron rod remained.

It was in this place, in the early 60's when Head strolled into the tale billed as the best fight *ever* in a town that puts great store in such claims. Like the best of epic stories, it is one of character and attitude, action strictly in a supporting role.

Head's opponent was equally as famous in other quarters. He hailed from a rival park known as Town Field. His name was Murphy, which one of the Murphy's, I couldn't say. There were about four of them, and each was the toughest kid around in in his respective age category. Their father was a semi-pro footballer who once played for the NFL. I suspect he still carried a grudge for being let go, and that might hold some clue as to the toughness of all the Murphy boys.

Beefed up with the Murphy muscles, Town Field was considered a tougher park. The Town Fielders also considered themselves better ball players, and a few of them, who knew some Wainwright boys from school, had arranged a game to be played at Wainwright.

Slightly ahead in the score, the visitors were getting loud when Head arrived on the scene. I remember one teller of the tale claimed to have actually been there when Head stepped onto his back porch. He told us that he'd spotted Head from the very beginning, slipping through the screen door. At first he just sat in a chair on the porch looking bored. Then he walked over to the railing. He listened to the trash talk and leaned over to see some of his friends being pushed about.

Below, the toughest of the Murphy boys had gotten the ball, and was leading the Town Fielders toward the hoop when Head, without use of his hands, jumped straight up onto the wooden railing of his porch. For a few seconds, he shifted about to maintain balance, and then looked down onto the court.

"Murphy," he said in a booming voice.

Below, Murphy stopped dribbling and looked upward, all players following his eyes.

Head then dove toward to the iron rod that surrounded the court, about 10 feet out and another 10 feet below. As he grabbed it, his weight dragged the wire down farther, and with it he swung out toward the court. Releasing the rod, he dropped onto the tarred surface, bending low directly in front of the man with the ball. As he straightened, his eyes remained on target.

"I hear you're tough," he said sticking that big noggin up to Murphy's face. I remember hearing the story with envy that first time as I sat on the Tranie's rough ground, thinking how rock-solid a compliment that would be coming from Head. Murphy only looked back at him. Then Head, leaned in closer, and pushed him.

They fought for about half an hour, each of them winning at different times. But, in the end, Head prevailed and the Town Fielders left without ever finishing the game. Each time I heard the story, no one could tell me the concrete details of the combat. Eventually, I realized that the "best fight" in Dorchester wasn't even about the fight. It was about a 17-year-old, eager to dive 30 feet down into a fight with one of the undisputed toughest kids in a town of 80,000, only to find out just how tough he was. That he defended the Park's name didn't hurt, either.

Another story, one that rivaled even Head's exploits, was that of the Indian; the one who died at the Quincy quarries. While not located in Dorchester, the quarries were one of its traditions. At the age of 13 up to the age of 15, jumping from quarry rocks was a rite of passage. About 10 miles from Dorchester, beyond a two- to three-hour hitchhiking journey, the quarries loomed over the Southeast Expressway. There, granite rocks had been carved from Quincy's earth to build the monument of Bunker Hill. Over the years, water eventually filled those forgotten holes. And centuries later, from the ledges of the cliffs surrounding the water, kids from all over Boston would jump. The more popular three of the quarry holes stood near the expressway. Of those, Suicide was the premiere, highest-ledged swimming hole.

During my own visits, I never saw anyone jump from Suicide's towering rock surfaces. To stare down into its void was to see and feel the heart of danger; at some points it dropped away 300 feet. When you threw a rock into the abyss, the rock appeared to move inward, toward the walls as it fell; and like most cliffs, Suicide had that mystical quality that made you slightly dizzy and pulling you toward it. The feared Table Top and Highway quarries were humble neighbors in the company of Suicide.

Separating Suicide from Table Top's 75-foot drop was an old, rusted iron bridge. Once it had served to ferry rock-stripping equipment; now, like an ancient artifact, it lay ignored. It was from that platform, it was said, the Indian jumped. When I finally made it to the quarries, I remember looking at the rusted iron, surrounded with the large gray chunks of quarry boulders, and the paths beyond that entered the woodlands. An Indian would have felt at home here, I thought. The sight of such nature awed those of us who had travelled the highways from the tarred streets and wooden three-deckers of home. But the Indian, I figured, might have enjoyed a more personal connection to the quiet wildness. Maybe that's what gave him the courage to try it.

Jumping from the highest points of quarry ledges, we would always toss a boulder in before us. This, we believed, "broke" the water, made it mushy, creating lesser resistance for those piercing its surface. We'd all heard about those who hit the unbroken hard water, lost their breath and drowned, or those whose pummeled bodies were pulled out. But from Suicide, there could be no softening of the water. To toss a boulder out past its protruding ledges would be difficult enough, and to hit your mark from such a height, near impossible. So the Indian had taken his own precaution: he brought a helmet with him. And then, on beautiful sunny day back sometime in the 50s, in the early days of rock and roll and black and white televisions, this Indian jumped.

With powerful legs he cleared all protruding obstacles on the way down. Knees high into his chest, he swung both arms out from his sides, circling the air with his hands, maintaining a steady balance. As he approached the water, he shot his legs straight down and brought the arms up, hugging his chest. His fists were clenched tight beneath his chin, as he sliced smoothly through the hard surface. And then, when the water rushed up past those fists, over the chinstrap, under the helmet, and around his head, he met his end.

That nylon chinstrap never did break; instead, it snapped his head clean off, as he continued into the water and the mythical tales told on street corners, the parks, and the Tranie in Dorchester.

I'd sit transfixed on the tar and rocks listening to the Indian's fate and hearing of others of the town's characters, such as Eddie Lilly's brother. Not content to swim around Tenean Beach's wooden barriers into the boat yard and lift a few bottles of booze, big brother decided to enjoy his booty on the spot. And later, on a roaring drunk, steered a yacht out of the yard. He was singing and still drinking whiskey when the Coast Guard caught him somewhere off the coast of Connecticut, or so I heard.

And there was Joey Mull, a character I would know only too well: he was always stirring up trouble and had an obsession for pranks. In a game of 'who can do the craziest thing,' he burned down his parents' summer cottage. On a couch he'd dragged to the front lawn, he drank beer from a cooler while cheering the fireman on; that is, before he was arrested.

Now, Billy Vision was a younger character, and different type. Billy didn't live in Dorchester, but he'd hitchhike 10 miles every day of the summer just to hang out there. The stories of Billy were of calmness under fire. We'd all heard the story of when three Lucky Strikes' rats stopped him to bum a cigarette one day. He gave it up freely, just part of his good nature. But when they surrounded him and asked, "how many cigarettes you got in that pack?" he just closed it up, and tucked the box back into his shirt pocket.

"Enough to fight for," he said, flashing the sincerest of smiles. After a few uneasy seconds, they all laughed. And Billy strolled away, down Dot Ave, cigarette pack in place.

No doubt similar stories of other characters and promising legends were being recounted all along Dorchester's corners and parks, each with their own home-grown heroes; some probably dead accurate, others not even close. The thirst for heroes is strong, as it should be. Paul Revere, John Adams, Hancock, they were Boston's official legends as they appeared in their revolutionary garb on the pages of our schoolbooks. But the British didn't roam Dorchester's streets any more. Kids like Murphy did, and it was kids like Head and Billy Vision who'd learned how to navigate those streets.

Such was the backdrop to the summer of '67 on the Tranie's pebbled surface, where we listened and learned the values of our town. It was the summer that took me, and the rest of the Lafield Street boys, into the new territory. The sense of adventure and danger of that hot season would never again be so acute.

Events of 1967

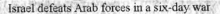

Israel defeats Arab forces in a six-day war

U.S. troops in Vietnam approach 500,000

The Summer Of Love kicks off with the first rock festival at Monterey, California, featuring The Who, Otis Redding, and the American debut of The Jimi Hendrix Experience

Antiwar protests continue to grow, climaxed by a march on the Pentagon in October

The Green Bay Packers defeat Kansas City in the first Super Bowl

The summer of love ends in violence; in Detroit 43 are killed, 1700 stores are destroyed. Race riots occur in 125 other cities.

The Beatles "Sgt. Pepper's Lonely Hearts Club Band" album wins the Grammy for "Album Of The Year," the first rock record given that award.

Three U.S. astronauts - Gus Grissom, Edward White and Roger Chaffee – die when their Apollo spacecraft burns in a simulated launch.

A draft board denies exemption for Mohammed Ali

CHAPTER VIII

THE PATH OF THE RIGHTEOUS

𝕴t was a tough park to play ball in. You could tell by the way the hard balls bounced, darting off to the sides, or suddenly springing up and smacking you in the face. There was too much rough dirt, pebbles, and rocks in the grass. That's what made the balls so erratic, so dangerous. It taught people bad moves, made them hesitant to move forward – toward the ball – no matter how loud the coach yelled. Reflexes are not good enough for a hard-hit ball on a bad bounce, and it hurt when that ball hit back.

Wainwright Park in the mid-60s had everything and everybody back then. As you approached it from the east side, you saw the basketball court first, which is where we 13-year-olds hung out. Beyond it was Charlie the Hunchback's little hovel. Charlie was the groundskeeper and was supposed to keep an eye on what was going on in the park. I'd see him in the mornings sometimes, and he'd look at me sternly as if he knew something I never could. But mostly, he stayed in that little brick building on the other side of the court.

The kiddie playground was just past Charlie's domain. Like the court, it too had its own chain-link fence. Young mothers chatted inside the perimeter as kindergarteners wandered about. Some adults stood on its tarred surface; others sat on the wooden benches, hunched forward, heads turned to each other. Kids climbed jungle bars, swung on swings, and stumbled dizzily from the spin-a-winner set, while mothers exhaled, and nodded their heads saying, *Iye, ain't it the truth*, or *Owe, yeah. I know about that.* Outside, to the left, spread the grassy section of the park. From the playground, on the far left and near right were two separate baseball diamonds. Kids were always running around those bases, or where the bases would have been, usually arguing about who was out and where the bases would have been.

Around it all towered a ten-foot high chain-link fence that kept the park isolated from the sidewalks, streets and the three-decker homes that ringed the area. Just inside that fence, the park ground dipped down imperceptibly toward the middle. In the winter, when the park flooded, the ice at the edges froze solid. When the air finally blew warm across its cold surface, that ice in the middle gave in first.

It began on the basketball court. Sully, about to be forced out of bounds, had whipped the ball hard off Sugar Bear, and laughed as it bounced out of bounds.

"Fucking little squirt. Try that again," said Sugar. Sully gave a devilish wide-mouthed smile and snickered his jagged laugh that went low, high, then low again. Even with three inches and about 20 pounds on Sully, Sugar resisted the impulse to strangle the little squirt for good reason.

"Uh oh, look at this," said Mull. I'd only spent a few weeks at Wainwright by this time, but already learned you had to keep an eye on Mull, a short loud mouth with a bowling-ball head. He seemed always on the scene when trouble arrived, usually in the background, his voice egging someone else on. He had a knack for steering clear of fights, getting others to make the moves for him.

Outside the fenced-in area, approaching the basketball court was an old guy, about 40. Behind him, head down, and looking like a little lost lamb, was surfer boy. The kid wore your basic flat sneakers and white socks, above them, the standard dungarees. His shirt, though, was definitely out-of-neighborhood material. It was light orange with a bunch of blurry colored circles on the front: it was a hippie shirt. Most noticeable was his long curly blonde hair. Anyone could see *this* kid had no problem with the girls.

"Shit," said Mull.

The old guy waved his hand forward. "Get up here," he instructed the boy. "Keep your head up," he added. His voice was clear, not angry, and his eyes were on us.

The kid's head snapped up, his pale cheeks looking even whiter against the pinkish cheekbone area. His teeth were clenched together and his eyes followed his father's gaze to where we had all stopped playing.

Moving slowly, Mull backed to the far side of the court, putting bodies between him and the old man. Like us, the surfer dude was somewhere around 13 years of age. Maybe it was the hair, or the shirt, or just because he looked too clean that made me think he was someone from a Beach Boy's tune.

"Is that them?" asked the old man, who now stood just short of the center entranceway of the basketball court. Sully held the ball loosely between his left arm and his side, fingers relaxed on the hand below, right hand on his hip. He was looking from the kid to the old man and back, on his face an amused smile. The rest of us watched the man, wondering what was about to happen.

"I told you before we left," answered the kid. "It was dark. I couldn't tell which ones it was. But it was three of these guys for sure."

This guy is crazy, I figured. There were about 20 of us inside the fence, outside, just him and the kid. I didn't like the kid, but even then, from the beginning, I wanted this to turn out OK for the guy. I wondered if I'd ever have the guts to do what he was doing. When he turned his head from his son, he was all business.

"All right," this time talking louder. "So you are the tough guys, huh? You are the ones who've been picking on my boy since we moved here. Well, all that's going to stop right here, right now." He said this slowly as though stating a fact, no hint of the threat. It was like directions – *you're going to go to the second stop light, and turn right.*

"Which ones of you did this to him?" he asked. He reached down to turn the boys face, but the kid stepped back, and then turned his face to the right. Below his left eye emerged a rough-shaped reddish bruise, and above it, some scrapes.

"He tells me it took three of you. Is that right?" He looked around. "Come on, you can talk." He studied our faces for a few seconds. "It took three of you tough guys to beat my boy?" He sounded truly disappointed in the lot of us as he said it. "Is that right?" he said again, this time his voice rising.

"That's right," answered the surfer, as though the question had been meant for him.

A bucket of guilt was being thrown over all of us. I studied the pale-faced kid, shooting his mouth off, while his old man took us all on. Donny Ives was among the tallest on the court, and he answered.

"Listen, mister. I don't know what happened to your son. But, you got no right blaming all of us." He glanced around the court. "I don't know who did that to him."

"Oh, so nobody knows what happened?" The old man had found someone in the crowd to confront and now he was going to have his say. "All of you," he said looking around. "All of you have been picking on my boy ever since we moved here. You're nothing but a bunch of pack rats." You could see the rhythm taking hold of him as he spoke. He was talking faster now, his voice picking up steam.

"You always have your buddies with you when you do something like this." He stopped to look around and then turned back to Donny. "Well, Harry here can take care of himself just fine when it's one on one. But that's not how pack rats fight. Is it?" We were shifting about now, looking among each other. I searched for guilt in anyone's face, wondering who might have started this, and who else knew. The man's words were having their intended effect.

"Like Donny said mister, we don't know what you're talking about," lied Mull. The old man didn't even look at him.

"You're just a bunch of cowards on your own. That's the way it always is." The old man was rubbing it hard into us. I sensed others too, felt on the wrong side of that fence; some looked down, others shook their heads. Then, from the sidelines, Sully let out a low, gurgling laugh. The man jerked his head one way, then the other; unable to spot who made the noise.

"That's funny. Funny? Huh!" he said, now angry. "OK, any of you, against my boy. All alone." With the words "my boy," the surfer dude glanced up at his father, then looked out toward us. It was like he was soaking up courage from the guy. "Who wants to prove me wrong?" the man asked.

No way that's going to happen, I thought. I took a few steps from the middle of the court to get a better look at this guy. I could sense half of us were already pulling for the kid, just for the old man's sake. He was doing all this, just for the kid.

"OK," came the voice from the sidelines. "You want someone to fight him. No problem." Sully, still wearing the quirky smile, lifted the basketball up with both hands and tossed it lightly back to Sugar. He walked toward the kid, ignoring the old man. "So where do you want to do this?"

The old man was obviously surprised by Sully's size. He stood at least three inches shorter than his son and was about 15 pounds lighter. The man looked over toward Donny, then Mulaney – the bigger boys.

"This is it? This is the one who'll fight?" he asked. *He wants a fair fight,* I thought, amazed. He didn't want his son to have the unfair size advantage.

Sully spoke, still looking only at the surfer.

"I'm one of the kids who kicked your ass last night," he said. "And I'd just as soon kick it again right now." He said it without fear, like he already knew the old man wouldn't do anything. Harry, looking back at him, started nodding his head.

"Yeah, I thought he was one of them. He is. He was one of them Dad." The old man's body stiffened as he looked down at Sully. It was easy to see he wanted to hit him, but he held back. "All right then," he said. "Over there. In the grass."

"Fucking A," said Sully, still looking only at the kid. "Let's play."

Walking the 75 feet across the grass, Sully seemed to be enjoying himself. I joined the small group gathered around him, trying to get a feel for what he was thinking. At his right shoulder was Mull.

"What you tell him for?" he asked. "He couldn't prove it was us." Sully was grinning and making a cackling sound that might be confused with giggling if not for the nasty edge in it.

Father and son were leading the way and approaching the middle ground between the two diamonds. They were about 20 feet in front of the outside ring of the gang. The old man was in the lead, walking head up, with surfer dude behind, looking straight ahead. He listened to last-minute instructions; some of it meant for all of us to hear. "Just a punk . . . remember what I said . . . only one this time . . . don't be afraid . . ." He said nothing wrong.

Sully was beaming with confidence and anticipation. His hair was a tangle of brown above a squat face, and his uneven teeth showed behind the stretched mouth. If he was putting on a show, it was a good one. In the middle of the crowd, he bathed in the attention. The idea that he might actually get hurt in a few moments seemed as far away as Hawaii, or somewhere else where that surfer dude's shirt belonged.

"OK," announced the old man. "This is good," he said, looking satisfied by the spacious middle area. "Are you ready over there?" he asked in our direction. The surfer had his fists clenched by his side now. His face had taken on a more reddish shade under the bruises and above that bright shirt. Sully was making jerking, laughing noises as loud as he could. They held no joy; they were just cackling sounds.

"You ready Sully?" someone finally asked.

"Ready? Yeah, I'm ready."

His face had turned serious, he was still and his eyes steady, as he looked straight at the kid, still ignoring the old man completely. Then he raised his left hand up toward his face. "Come on over," he said, pulling his four fingers inward. "Over here pussy."

The kid glanced at his father. For the first time, the old man looked a bit uneasy. He kept his eyes on Sully and motioned forward with one hand. "Go ahead son." The boy walked hesitantly toward us. His eyes were on Sully's as we made space for him. When he got about 10 feet away, we spread around, loosely surrounding the two. The park, it seemed, had shrunk to just that circle, with only us on the perimeter and the two about to meet in the middle.

I wondered how many others there, like me, were hoping the kid could pull it off. *Damn, he should be able to*, I thought. He was bigger, stronger, and not too afraid. But with every step from the old man, he had moved slower. We fanned out, widening the circle, everyone getting a ringside view. Sully, who had been so loud moments before, now only stared at the kid. He would not speak again until the fight was over. He raised his fists like a boxer, peered out over them, and then charged directly at the surfer.

The kid stood his ground and put his fists and elbows up front, instinctively leaning forward to absorb the rush. Sully's right arm went back during his run and he shot it out toward the kid's face just as they were about to collide. At the same time he threw the punch, he jumped into the air. The punch went off the kid's arms and over his head, the weight of Sully's body slamming up around the kid's chest. He didn't hit him where he wanted, but the body slam sent him to the ground. Sully was on top off him now in the dirt, both hands flailing. The kid was grunting and breathing loudly. For about ten seconds, they fought, the kid mostly fending off punches, trying desperately to grab a hold of the arms. He finally succeeded.

He managed to pin the arms to Sully's sides and he was trying to roll on top of him. His left eye was half closed and blood ran from his nose. But, he fought on, not panicking. He arched his body, pulling, and it looked he had a chance, after all. Then his voice let out a shock of pain.

"Augghh! He's biting me Dad. He's biting me."

I turned toward the old man, expecting to see him jumping onto Sully. He had moved within the circle, his fists, again, clenched tight. But still he held back.

"All right son," I heard in measured words. "Bite him back. If he's going to bite you, you bite him back."

But Sully had got his right arm free and it was all he needed. His legs had crept around the kid's legs and he was punching him rapidly with his free fist. After taking about four solid shots, the kid managed to roll away. Sully scrambled quickly after him, but overshot his mark as the kid pushed him. Sully took the shove, rolled over, and came up on his feet. The surfer, who should have moved faster, was coughing and shaking his head to get dirt off him. By the time he moved to get up, Sully stood above him. From his sitting position, the kid lurched to the side to jump up. But Sully's first kick took a leg from under him. Then the kid made another mistake.

Instead of rolling around, grabbing for legs, or somehow scrambling to get back to his feet, he started to cover up. His hands went up by the sides of his face and he pulled his knees inward. The next kick caught him in the ribs, then another off his arms into the neck. In between kicks, Sully did an awkward two-step to maintain his balance. His mouth was stretched wide and his eyes bulged as he looked for places to hurt. The kid was covering his sides pretty good, so Sully lifted his leg and stomped down on his chest.

"He's kicking me dad," the kid yelled.

If it was one of us down there, a friend would have jumped in and tried to end it. Some kids had crowded in close to the old man, and he pushed them back.

"Then you kick him son," he said. "You kick him back."

And just how the hell is he supposed to do that? I thought. I couldn't believe the old man would even say it. Sully kicked the kid one more time somewhere around the neck and the surfer was done. He rolled over, his arms relaxed and his head fell to the side. Sully, though, was still moving. He circled around the kid, in the direction he had rolled after that last kick. As he drew back his leg, I heard myself and two or three others yell, "NO!" No thoughts had been involved in the reaction, just a powerful sense of unfairness.

Sully looked up, the area around his eyes crinkled in disbelief. Our eyes locked for about three seconds, till I felt a flush of shame. As his eyes moved to find the others who had yelled, I felt the heat on my face and wondered, why had I blushed?

At the time, there was only instinctual shame. In his eyes, I saw that he knew, beyond any doubt, that he was right. The forcefulness of that look stopped me cold, till the blood raced to the skin of my face. It was him, and no one else, that stood there bruised and cut from the effort of fighting a bigger, stronger foe. Who, those eyes asked? Who dared tell him now what he could and couldn't do? There was righteousness in those eyes.

Then he looked down at the kid. He did not rush this time; there was no need. A full second before the act, I felt deadened. I don't know how the old man managed it, but still he held back. He would not compromise: his son would fight his own fights. Sully soaked in the moment, picked his spot and then kicked that kid dead in the center of his forehead.

"Satisfied?" he said. He barely looked up at the man standing there motionless, before walking off. The guy watched him for a few seconds, then his hands opened up, and he walked over to his son.

What could he say to him now, I thought. Would he tell him he fought a good fight; that he was proud of him for fighting fair? I felt anger, and pity. He had done what he thought was right. He was brave and did everything he could to pour that into his boy. He wanted to teach the kid to fight his own fight, and fight fair. Only if the other guy broke the rules first, could he. He was determined to get the boy on that straight path. *He was right,* I tried to believe. But everything, everything in my body told me he was wrong.

Heading back to the basketball court with Mull and a few others, Sully laughed about the blood.

"Hey, they're new sneakers," he said, stopping close to Charlie's empty stairs. He stuck out his right foot to show his prize. The sneaker had a thick sole and a rubbery tip that came back over the toes. On the tip was a faint smear of blood, more pink than red. "I needed to break them in anyway," he said. He and Mull laughed as though that was the funniest thing they'd ever heard.

Movies of 1967

Bonnie and Clyde

Cool Hand Luke

The Graduate

The Dirty Dozen

Guess Who's Coming to Dinner

Barefoot in the Park

In the Heat of the Night

Casino Royale

To Sir With Love

Valley of the Dolls

Camelot

In Like Flint

The Taming of the Shrew

Up the Down Staircase

Point Blank

CHAPTER IX

SKY PILOT

The golden haired one earned the name Sky Pilot because of his taste for flying. The wandering high-tailed cat didn't take to the air under his own power; his adopted comrade – Mike Columbo – who'd named him after a popular song of the time, tossed him wildly upward.

"Watch this," Mike began the routine, cigarette sticking out of the left side of his mouth, bending to lift Sky. His eyes widened as he lifted his little friend. He lowered and raised him twice more before launching Sky about 12 feet into the air. Before the screeching cat's feet hit the ground, Mike's cigarette was back in his hand. The cat sprang back up, his tail rising three-quarters of the way rigid straight before floating backward, hairs catching the breeze.

"Watch him," Mike continued as he kept his eye on the feline. Slowly Sky circled and stretched his long, front legs forward, and then pulled himself back over to the one who would toss him again. Rubbing against the legs, he purred and waited. A few of us told Mike to knock it off.

"I tell you, he likes it," Mike insisted. But when Kevin and a few others pointed out that it was just a matter of time before the cat would get hurt, he let Sky be.

About five-foot five, carrying a larger gut than most of us, Mike was slightly smaller and a little heavier than average. Ever since the Beatles showed up on Ed Sullivan a few years back, everyone was growing hair longer. Mike's was the longest. From the back of the right side of his head, it grew forward in a 45-degree angle, slanting down across the narrowing base.

Mike was no regular on any street corner; he liked to cover ground, wandering around Dorchester looking for action or just checking out what was going on where. When we were at Lafield, he'd join us for a day or two, or week or two, as the mood hit him, showing up at odd times with new stories of adventure and entertaining us with newly discovered jokes.

It wasn't until I joined the rest of the Lafield Boys at Wainwright Park that I learned Mike was a regular visitor there, too. I was even more surprised that he actually hung out with some of the older kids at the park.

On a Sunday trip to a local bowling alley – Ten Pin – one day, Kevin and I bumped into him. He was with Billy Savage and Stevie Mull's older brother, Joey, the character known for pranks. Aside from being a prankster, Joey also had a reputation for discipline problems at Saint Mark Elementary School, holding the record for being sent home most often. Two years older than the rest of us, he'd already been picked up for separate incidents of drinking and stealing. It was still a few years before he'd burn down his parent's cottage, though. Billy with his freckled rough face suffered under the reputation of an older brother, a well-known tough guy and promising future felon. Without that burden, I suspect Billy would've had a nicer life. But with everyone he met expecting his famous brother's tough-guy persona, poor Billy sometimes had to work a side of him he didn't really relish.

"Come on, come on, sing for me," hushed Mike to the *Spin-A-Winner* game. Ignoring the alley rules, the ever-present cigarette stuck out of the side of his mouth opposite the manager's desk. Slamming his hand straight down on the pinball machine's right metal corner, he sent just enough vibration to the inside bumper to bounce the silver ball back on course toward the flippers. But when his belly push slid the legs backward, the lights flared and the musical chimes went wild.

"Damn," was all Mike said. Although he easily got more free games out of those Ten Pin machines than anyone I knew, he also tilted them more often than anyone else. I suspect now that he just liked to hear the bells go off.

After Kevin and I mumbled our hello's to the others and talked to Mike for a bit, he steered us toward a couple of the easier machines to beat, and later on, the five of us headed back in the direction of the Saint Mark schoolyard. We never did get that far.

"Let's check out the new cars," Joey said as we were leaving the parking lot. He jerked his head toward the car dealership next door.

On the walk, Billy talked a lot to Kevin and I, making me think he was as uncomfortable around Joey as the both of us. It was an odd combination: Joey, the uncontrollably wild one; Mike, who fed off wildness; and Billy, the reluctant wild one.

Outside the dealer's show room, nose against the glass window and hands cupped around the sides of his face, Mike spotted something inside. When he spoke, the pitch of his voice relayed awe.

"Holy Shit!" he said in a hushed voice.

Inside, I saw only cars none of us could afford. But Mike's vision had gone beyond them to a grey metal box up on the wall, its foot-long door half open.

"Joey!" he yelled. "Do you see it?" When nobody answered, Mike added. "That box. It's always supposed to be locked." Kevin and I looked at each other and shrugged.

"See those keys?" Mike was talking slow now. "The ones on the left?"

"What do you got, Mikee?" Joey responded, apparently as blind to the opportunity as the rest of us.

"Those are Master Keys," Mike answered, saying the words like someone might whisper, *the gates of heaven.* "They'll start any car on this lot," he said. "And lots of other cars."

Only one problem remained: those keys were still on the inside of a locked door. And without Joey, it would have ended right there. But when Joey heard those words of promise, he became determined to own those keys. Kevin, Billy and I wanted no part of it, so Joey had us stand guard by the parking lot. I don't mean to say it was that easy a choice – that we just decided to go along with Joey. We knew it was a mistake from the beginning, but to say no would have brought everlasting shame on us – labeled cowards by one of the older kids from the park, a park we'd just joined.

Before we separated, Kevin and I spoke quietly. We agreed that Joey would probably get us all thrown in jail, and tried to figure out how to get out of this thing. Although Joey was older, he was only as tall as Kevin and I. With a fleshy, large face, short brown hair, and bulky shape, he outweighed us by about 30 pounds. Some of it might've been muscle, but most of it was fat. I could never put my finger on it, but there was definitely something off kilter inside Joey. From the few times I'd observed him, I saw he wasn't happy unless someone else wasn't, and danger was always involved. I figured he was either missing something natural, or had too much of something unnatural.

The three of us spread out at the corners of the parking lot, mostly to keep an eye on the folks exiting Ten Pin; we'd warn Joey and Mike if anyone walked in our direction. Instead of a casual walk home, I was now sweating out the possibility that both Kevin and my lives could change drastically in a moment. Jail may not have been a big concern to Joey, but it sure was to us. And everyone who stepped out of Ten Pin, and every glance in our direction, triggered a rush of blood. No one ever came in our direction, and in about 10 minutes we were called back. Both Joey and Mike had keys in hand. "Come with me," Joey ordered. The plan was to just drive some cars around the lot to see how fast they were, and then leave them there undamaged. I had a sense of doom before I even closed the car door behind me, and things went wrong right away. Billy, goofing around, made the big mistake of the night, jumping on the hood of our car.

"What's this fool doing?" asked Joey.

I agreed. With folks still exiting Ten Pin, Billy was drawing attention to our illegal activities. But Billy, blind to the danger, had stretched across the whole front windshield, looking inside the car and grinning like he was posing for a home movie. That was when Joey eased into that off-kilter place. The advance warning I got was just two words.

"Hold on," he said flatly.

His foot was revving the engine loud in neutral gear when his hand moved to the stick on the steering column. When he popped it into drive, Billy's face began to transform from one of silly joy, to concern, to absolute terror. In those three seconds the car reached enough speed to tell Billy he was about to get seriously hurt.

"What are you doing?" I yelled. We were headed for a chain link fence about 50 yards away. Less worried about Billy now than that fence smashing through the front windshield, I leaned forward to look into Joey's face: he was in a semi-trance. I reached for the car's door handle and considered – jump, or brace for the hit. But before I could decide, Joey stopped me with a single word.

"Ready?" he said. It wasn't so much the word that froze me, but the way he said it – with a complete sense of calmness.

He put his hand beneath the stick shift, and hesitated slightly as though to soak in the moment. In a quick glance I saw Billy yelling and desperately grabbing at the smooth surface of the windshield up toward the roof. It was then when Joey popped the shift up into Neutral, and then again, right into reverse. With the roar of the engine and the screeching tires, I thought the car was going to blow up. For maybe half a second I believed Billy still had a chance.

The tires high squeal gave voice to Billy's panic. But Billy never did get that grip on the window or roof. He just started to roll sideways down the length of the hood. There was no way he had time to prepare for the fall: he was flipping too fast. I didn't know it at the time, but the hood ornament ripped a hole in his denim pants and right leg just before he went flying off the car and across the ground. About 40 feet back, Joey hit the brakes. With a half smile on his face, he glanced over to me. Then he popped the stick shift downward again, "pop, pop." By the time it popped into drive, the pedal must have been all the way down, and the tires began screeching again.

For some reason, I sensed he wanted me to go for wheel. He could have blamed me for distracting him, causing Billy to be run over. My hand was already on the door handle, so I pulled it and jumped out. Billy was still laying out there beyond my view, but I was pretty sure that look of terror was back on his face as the car lurched forward, screaming toward him.

The wheels squealed once more, just before the car skidded to within five feet of Billy.

By the time I got there, Kevin and Mike had already arrived. They wanted to know what happened. Since I hadn't yet worked that out in my own head, I just looked to Joey. "Forget it," was all he said.

It took a while, but Mike finally convinced Joey that someone needed to take Billy to a hospital. His leg was bleeding hard from the small hole in it. When Joey finally conceded, he put together some story for Billy to tell the doctors about how "the accident" happened, tossing in heavy threats if Billy were to stray from the script. After all, Joey reminded him, he had hit the brakes the second time even though Billy didn't deserve it, after he had brought the unwanted attention. In Joey's eyes, he was the reluctant leader who had done what was right for all of us and actually taught Billy a useful life lesson. Selfless, and generous to a fault, God bless him. I doubt Billy had the same view, but was in no position to argue.

Kevin, Billy, and I made it a point to stay well clear of Joey after that day. I thought Mike had too, until a month later at the park. Sully, who had spent time with them, told us of their more recent adventure.

The two of them and Sully had travelled to the largest shopping store within walking distance – Orbits. As Sully began the story, it became clear Joey had adopted Mike as a protégé, and the day's lesson was shoplifting.

On the road to Orbits, Joey coached them both. They were to enter the store at different times. Once inside, Mike and Joey would take turns following each other from a distance. Joey already knew some of the store detectives by sight, but this would allow them to spot any others that might take an interest in them. Joey also told Mike that he wanted a watch, and Mike was going to get it for him. Sully was to stay clear and only get involved if he saw a detective approaching the watch counter.

Between occasional gulps of beer, Sully recounted how the plan went down; his quirky smile a clear tipoff that it hadn't gone well.

After walking around the store for a while, Joey met Mike in an aisle farther away. He then led Mike to the watch display counter and signaled which watch he wanted. Then they headed back to the aisle.

"Joey wanted some watch on the very bottom shelf," Sully explained. In order for Mike to get it, he'd have to reach completely over the waist-high counter, then down to almost the floor, then into the display case to grab hold of it. Mike was telling Joey there were much nicer watches on the first and second counter. "I don't even know if I can reach that bottom row," Mike complained. But Joey was adamant. He reassured Mike, telling him that he would get him plenty of time to reach it by keeping the lady behind the counter busy.

At the park, Sully stopped to take another gulp of beer, giving us all time to take in the scene. When he lowered the can, he looked around to each of us, making sure we had the picture.

Sure enough, Joey became the politest kid in the store and asked the watch clerk if she would get out one of the watches from the second shelf. Joey held the watch and started asking questions about it as Mike, on the opposite side, began the reach-over.

Not bothering to drink this time, Sully just scanned our faces before continuing.

"He was way up on his toes completely over the counter, stretching for Joey's watch," Sully said. It took Mike a few tries with his fingertips to drag the watch toward his hand. And just when he got a hold of it, Joey stopped talking to the lady, and pointed straight at Mike, yelling.

"'Hey, what's *he* doing?'"

The lady spun around to the stunned look on Mike's face as he was rising up, watch in hand.

"He's a thief!" Joey yelled as though astonished, loud enough for everyone in the store to hear. "Stop him."

Then he started running toward Mike. Through the store Mike ran, Joey behind him yelling. "Stop that boy. He's a thief." All the way out the store and up Victory Road Joey chased him, yelling. When he finally caught up to him, Joey fell on the ground laughing.

At the park, some were laughing; others were more wide-eyed. Sully swore it was all true, though. He said he had run after Joey like he was trying to help catch the thief, too. The store detectives fell behind, and quit running halfway across the parking lot. When Sully caught up, he said Joey was still laughing and Mike was trying to catch his breath. Mike was mad, at first, Sully said. But later he shook his head at Joey, and told him he was just crazy.

"Joey wasn't that bad," Sully insisted. "He let Mike keep the watch he stole." Sully then reached for his pocket as though he was going to pull something out. "'This is the one I really wanted anyway,' Joey told Mike." You could see the admiration in Sully's face. "He'd pocketed the watch the lady handed him."

It seemed the more I visited the park, the more I heard of how Mike was getting into trouble. From Mike's friend, Benny, I heard how Mike's mother found out he'd been tapping into a bottle of her boyfriend's rum. Mike had been taking portions of the rum and replacing it with water. Eventually, the boyfriend, Chubby, came by and asked for a rum and coke, and ended up drinking something more like water and coke, which he spit into the apartment sink.

That was just another of the unusual things about Mike – he was the only one of us who lived in an apartment, not a three-decker. Of course, he didn't have a father, either, at least not one who lived at home.

With his mother still in her 30's, we all figured she was divorced, a rarity in Dorchester back then.

To make ends meet, she ran her own flower shop, which is where she met Chubby. Only about five foot, five, with a round figure, Chubby was one of her best customers. He did something – nobody knew what – in Boston's Italian North End section, and was always buying flowers for funerals of other Italian guys. Although Chubby was someone who liked to laugh, Mike had a talent for getting him mad. And after Chubby spit that drink into the sink, he lit into both his girlfriend and her trouble-making son.

Not long after the rum incident, Mike ended up at Dorchester's Police Station 11. I can't remember what he did to get there; but whatever it was, it couldn't have been as bad as what happened afterward. Benny told the story.

"When we first got there, two cops started grilling the both of us," said Benny. A few inches taller than the rest of us, and heavy like a bear, Benny told his stories alternating from slow and quiet to waving his arms around wildly. He started out quietly.

"Mike started crying like crazy, saying how he was going to get into all kinds of trouble when he got home."

It was a slow night at the park, and there were only three or four of us there. Still, some of us were surprised to hear about the crying. It seemed like something Benny might have left out. But the crying was just the beginning.

The two policemen who picked Mike up had already questioned him and decided to let him go. They weren't going to press charges or send him to juvenile detention; they just wanted to talk to his mother before letting him out.

Benny was showing little emotion, relaying the story almost like he was making a report. It was hard to figure out where he was going.

He told us how Mike's Mom walked in, looking good, all dressed up.

"But she wasn't smiling," said Benny. It seemed the phone call home had interrupted plans with Chubby and he had gone home pissed off about her brat kid ruining another date.

When someone asked how he knew that, Benny looked annoyed, but answered that Mike had told him later. I wondered how much of the story we were hearing came from Benny's eyes and how much he got from Mike.

Benny didn't say much more about what Mike's mother was wearing, only that they were nice. He probably didn't know, and didn't say, anything about the kind of day she'd had that day. I can't help thinking it was probably a tough one. Maybe she'd had to deal with a lot of picky customers who didn't like the colors of her flowers. Maybe she didn't pull in enough for the bill payments that month. I don't know. I knew she'd been working hard trying to make a life for the both Mike and herself, and maybe she just got tired of getting the short end of that deal. Maybe that's why she did what she did.

When Benny told us what she said, he finally came alive, jerking his arms around quickly.

"Why are you guys calling me? I can't do anything about him. He don't listen to me. Not to anything I say," she screamed at the cops. Mike was on his feet trying to calm her down.

"It's OK, Ma, I'm OK. It was nothing. Let's go."

"Go!" she'd looked at him like he was a stranger. "Go where?" she glared. "You're not going anywhere. You're not coming home with me! What for? So you can get in more trouble? Cause me more problems? I've had it Michael. I'm done." Then she'd turned to the cops.

"So what are you guys going to do?" She demanded. "Can't you send him someplace?"

Benny quieted down again when he talked about the cops. He said they just looked at each other, like they didn't know what to do. Then the tall one went to her and tried to get her out of the room to talk privately.

That was when she started in about the cars, said Benny. He wasn't jerking his hands around like before and his voice wasn't as loud. He just said the words, pausing in between sentences.

"You know, he steals cars," she began. "All the time . . . He's even got Master Keys."

It had grown dark in the park. I realized I was no longer looking at Benny, just down at the ground. I think we all were.

She dug into her purse, "God knows where or how he got these. I got them now, though. Here," she yelled, pulling the ring of keys out. "Now, what are you guys going to do? I've had it with him. I'm not kidding here. I've had it. Here are the keys. So what? What now?" she yelled.

One of the policemen took the keys, and all four of them just looked at her.

"We just looked," Benny said. "Me, and the cops and Mike. We didn't say anything." Benny's voice was insistent, like he was defending himself. Those of us listening were pretty quiet, too.

"Then she started crying," Benny said. After a few seconds, I think we all looked up together, hoping there was more to the story. But there wasn't.

Mike spent two months on the juvenile detention farm. His own mother had turned him in. Hell, she could have beaten him half to death, or let Chubby do it. We could all understand that. But having your own mother turn you over to the cops, send you away to a place where you got treated like dirt, and everyone was trouble. That was something I don't believe any of us wanted to think about.

After the summer, I saw Mike was back bouncing from corner to corner, and like his old high-tailed friend, still looking for excitement wherever he could find it, with whoever could provide it.

Over the years I went off to the military and lost track of Mike. On one trip home, I heard that he'd taken his own life. Everyone I told said they already knew that. Nobody knew how he did it, and nobody knew why.

CHAPTER X

TRAPPED

I was halfway through the summer of '67 when the police car pulled over in an angle in front of me, my heart jumping toward my Adam's apple. I'd been hitchhiking by the side of the road, my remaining sneaker wrapped up tight in the towel tucked under my left arm, and my comrades sitting by the curb. The car had been cruising behind a string of traffic so I didn't spot it till it careened around me, cutting off any escape from the Milton corner toward home.

"Hold it right there, fellas," yelled the policeman who'd jumped out the passenger door. Behind me Sully and Mull had scrambled to their feet.

I knew in that instant, there was no escape. Even if I bolted away in my bare feet and managed to get away, one of us would be caught, most likely Mull, and he'd spill his guts.

We'd spent the day at the Milton Quarries, jumping from the cliff edges of the smaller quarries into the warm water below. None of the jumps were higher than 25 feet, though the most dangerous was a smaller 20-foot drop into water. Beneath its surface were two rows of dark shadows: each indicated stacked cars. They'd been stolen and dumped there, or just dumped there and reported stolen, we'd learned. We also heard of the kid who had jumped from its ledge without sneakers: a car antenna had gone straight up his leg, coming out where his knee bent.

On the opposite side of the quarry, Kevin and I played a game of chasing the can. We stood on a ledge about five feet up. After filling a soda can with water, we'd toss it into the water, count a few seconds, and then dive in after it. We'd worked our way up to five-second delays, going two to three full strokes beneath the surface to retrieve the can. It was a fun game till Stevie Mull came by.

Mull was his usual smart-aleck self, walking around, looking for the right buttons to push. The first time I had ever seen Mull was just a few years before I joined the park. He was with the older Wainwright boys who had staged an impressive show of force on the way to teach Tom Savage, Billy's older brother, a lesson.

I'd been sitting on my Lafield Street front porch when about 30 kids came strutting down the street like the circus had come to town. Most of those at the front were 15 – 17 years old. The parade was spread out, about three to four kids across, with the line 25 feet deep. In shorts or dungarees, most had t-shirts on, though some wore no shirts at all. Near the front, one carried a baseball bat; another waved a block of wood. Three rows from the front, not within the mob, but out a few feet, strutted mull. He looked like a court jester, laughing and yelling things like "Yeah, there's going to be some trouble now . . . look out everybody . . . we're coming!" When he spotted Kevin, Archie, and I up on the porch, he yelled out. "What are you looking at? You want trouble?" We were all pretty amazed at the scene before us and said nothing. When he yelled toward us again, one of the older kids told him to shut his mouth. We were obviously too young to hold his interest.

As it turned out, Tom was not home when they got to his house, so they turned around and went back to the park, cheering each other as though they'd won some epic battle. I remember thinking that they must have been pretty scared of Tom to bring that many people to the fight. Whether it was to be a one-on-one or just a free-for-all, I never learned.

"What kind of pussy game is that?" Mull asked. Pussy was one of Mull's favorite words. He used it like an animal tamer would a whip, or a chair, steering the dumb animals in the direction he wanted. When I taunted him to dive in himself, he ignored me. Instead, he offered to throw the can, then tossed it out too far for either Kevin or I to reach; of course, that was just a mistake.

After we filled up another can, he talked me into waiting up to seven seconds, and then he stepped in my way as I went for the edge. Bumping him out of the way, I dove through the water. Below, I could only see a sparkle of sun on the top of the can five full feet down. It was slipping slowly toward the total darkness beneath. I knew I'd be going much deeper than I'd ventured before, but felt a need to do it. Four strokes later I caught it just as I descended into the sub-surface ice water. Waving both hands while holding onto the can I was still shocked from my first encounter with the freezing water and completely out of breath when I broke the surface.

Up on the rock Mull's excited voice told me he was impressed that I'd gone so deep. But I knew he didn't really care about that. He'd gotten me to do something I shouldn't, tricked me into working against my own self-interest. It seemed everything he said or did to anyone could be traced back to that motive. When Kevin asked why I let him talk me into things, I had no answer. At the time, his ability to get folks to do his bidding was to me some type of mysterious power, something akin to what an old Indian medicine man might have possessed.

I had no clue back then and wouldn't have known how to say it anyway, but Mull was, if not the first, the cleverest manipulator I had the misfortune to encounter. At an early age, he'd mastered how to manage and use people for his own entertainment. And even when I started to pick up on the secrets of his dark act, he still knew the right buttons to push.

Coming back from the quarries, the eight of us had cut through a trail behind a schoolhouse. First Mull started on Sully and Flannery, how they couldn't even reach the schoolhouse with a rock, much less hit a window. Then he turned to a few others, taunting us with how we didn't have the balls to even try it. He tossed the first rock, which was way off the mark. Within minutes, we were all throwing rocks, and the next thing I knew, two cops were chasing us down the trail. That was when I ran right out of my left sneaker. When I turned to go back for it, I saw one of the cops coming on fast, so I took off again in the one sneaker. At the end of the trail everyone scattered in different directions. Sully and Mull had followed me, and we ended up thumbing home together.

By now, the second cop had come around the car and was looking at my towel and smiling.

After he listened to our story about how we were coming from somewhere else, and – for sure – not the Milton Quarries, he told me to unwrap the towel. When I did, he went back to his car and brought out my other sneaker.

"Looks like a match, don't it?" was all he said.

Thirty minutes later, we pulled up to Sully's house. Up front, the cops were debating whether or not to let us go. A few minutes ago, they were definitely going to take us all home. But when they heard Sully's full name, they got nervous. One of them turned and looked at him. "Is your father . . ." he started. But Sully never let him finish.

"Yeah, he's a policeman too," said Sully. "He's works downtown Boston."

Sully watched for the cop's reaction when he finished. I too saw the cop's face freeze, eyebrows stretching upward. He looked steadily at Sully as though first asking, and then sharing, an unspoken moment of understanding. The other cop had jerked his head back when Sully spoke, and then looked over at his partner. They talked low after that, but I could still hear some of it. The driver was all for letting us go, but his partner talked about a report, and held up a clipboard and paperwork. Then he turned back toward Sully.

"I really don't want to do this to you kid," he said, like he meant it. "But we're going to have to take you inside."

The way Sully nodded his head, and the way the cop shrugged, it looked like home was a worse option than jail. How bad is Sully's Dad, I wondered, if even two cops were afraid to knock on his door? I was certain back then that the cops were afraid of what Sully's father might do to them: now, I'm pretty sure they were more likely worried about what would happen to Sully.

Sully's full name was William Sullivan. Other than the nuns, no one called him William, though. Only on rare occasion did anyone call him Billy. Sully didn't like it when people acted like they knew him. I'd already witnessed what he'd done to that kid in the park, and figured, pound for pound, he was the toughest kid around. Still, I could never decide who was more dangerous: him, or Mull.

Before going to Sully's door, the cops pushed us for the names of the other kids. I pleaded truthfully that I was new to the crowd, and didn't know any of the kid's last names. Mull and Sully gave up two names. The only one I remember is Billy Vision's. I remember because

107

years later, Billy told me that Sully and Mull reported that I was the one who gave up his name. Knowing them well enough, Billy told me he never bought their story. While one cop stayed with us, the other went to the door with Sully. When he returned, he shook his head side to side while looking at his partner, saying nothing. Afterwards, they dropped off Mull.

Fortunately my father wasn't home when the cops brought me in. One of the cops sat on the couch in my front room and told my mother how I was with the gang that broke four windows in the Milton school. His partner, still outside, couldn't find a parking space so he just stayed in the car in the middle of the street with the motor running for five minutes, about four minutes more than it took to get the entire neighborhood's attention. Then my mother worked me over good, laying enough guilt on me to last the rest of the summer. She talked about the shame. God knows what she suffered just to end up with a criminal like me on her hands. She hit me over the head with the personal disappointment – a fine example I was to my younger brothers. The barrage continued with the irreparable harm done to the family name. How could she, or any member of the family, look any neighbor in the eyes again? She ended with "I just hope your father never finds out."

That made two of us.

In my room later, I had plenty of time to think. I tried to figure out why I'd been doing so many things lately that gave me pain, and no pleasure. I remembered the games of Lafield Street being ones of challenges, or tests of skills. Even with Ramzee lurking around, the old street came back to me as a paradise, a haven of fun. I began to realize how the park's games were different. They were tainted with a sinister intent behind them.

I remembered how a few weeks earlier the gang had even given a kid a new name. Steve, one afternoon, became Monk; it wasn't because he was religious, but because he climbed a fence as fast as a monkey. Everyone called him Monk now. He was being humiliated for having done something well. I remember how I hesitated at first to call him by the name; and later, how hurt he looked when I did. There were people out there, I began to realize, that could change you, even change your name too.

It was a scary to realize I could be controlled, led places I didn't want to go. I had already disgraced the family forever, and I couldn't even explain to myself why. I felt again like that lost two year old, stumbling across a large room where giants spoke words only they understood; and me, struggling to just stay on my feet.

CHAPTER XI

THE WALL

Ned, Kevin, Sully and I were standing in a gentle breeze on "The Wall," a cliff that stared 50 feet down onto the hard, still surface of quarry water. Ned was the veteran on that warm, summer day. He'd enticed all of us along with visions of high jumps, deep water, roving gangs and other dangers. An hour of thumbing had brought us to the rocks that would test our courage.

More than a century earlier, in 1826, workers for the city of Quincy had carted rocks from the quarries to Charlestown to build The Bunker Hill Monument, a towering obelisk built to commemorate the rebellious spirit of a young country. The quarry rocks left that site on the country's first railroad system. This is the history of the Quincy quarries as the tourists in the downtown cable cars hear it.

To those of us from Dorchester, the spirit of the quarries was what was left behind, after those rocks had been ripped out – the plunging holes through the hard granite and the deadly pits of water below. It was a place where major gangs, like the Devil's Disciples, drank beer. It was where boys, schooled on city streets, ventured to climb closer to manhood. Nobody knew for sure how many jumpers had drowned in its cold waters, but more than a few bodies had been recovered from the underwater ledges, and would be again. It was a place where gangs held an uneasy truce, not bothering each other. The swimming holes were set in almost hallowed ground, and everyone who went there had to jump or not go again. If you made at least one jump, it was enough; but the higher, the better.

Cliffs that ranged from two to 300 feet in height surrounded the Quincy's quarries' three main swimming holes. That day, we'd already walked the trails from the Highway quarry, skirted Suicide, and stood before Tabletop.

This quarry had a horseshoe shape, formed by cliffs on three sides. We stood on the right side of the horseshoe, the side called The Wall, facing across to the other leg with the opening on our right. That was where the cliffs dwindled down to the ground and the water bounced up onto a rocky shore. On our left, a 20-foot wide patchwork of earth and rocks led to a rusted iron bridge. The bridge separated Tabletop from Suicide. Legend had it, that was where "The Indian" had last jumped a decade before.

Atop The Wall, I watched jumpers from the water's edge begin their climb. Others had circled the quarry in the wood line and stared down at the water, working up their courage to jump. This was a secluded place, a picture of an earlier time: the crushed-grass paths through the wood line; the trees, mostly pine, but with a sampling of oak and gum; the giant boulders with streaks of mineral red; and the sun reflecting off the water's black surface.

As we turned to our right and began walking along the quarry, we saw the only sign of a modern world present there. Halfway across

The Wall lay five painted red footsteps. From the right they came at an angle toward us, the last shape of a foot perched at the very edge of the cliff. Blind to their deadly significance, I stepped lightly over them and continued on.

"What's the big deal?" I had asked Ned when he first challenged us with the quarries. "You jump off rocks and you land in the water. How hard is that?" That, of course, was weeks before Kevin, Sully, or I had seen any thing like Tabletop's dangerous cliffs and The Wall's blood-red markings.

In the nature of the quarries, our home lives paled, as though this was the real world, not the city streets and three-deckers we'd left behind. In our homes at night, my friends and I watched images of gunfire and wounded soldiers being carried away on stretchers, and policemen clubbing protesters before dragging them away. It was a wild time that caused all of us to think, and occasionally talk about, our own level of guts. And here, Ned had presented us with a measuring stick. How brave are you? How high up the cliffs would you climb and jump before fear froze you to a ledge? There was adventure and the dread, and each of us with chances to confront our own limits of fear. It was simple, and it was measurable.

The day had started easy enough on the lower ledges; it was as I had thought, you jump and you land in water. But, at the 25-foot mark, the adrenaline kicked in. Our bodies sensed danger, tightening our chests and sending our blood racing. When you start to lean in the air, it's a helpless feeling, and the more time you spend in the air, the more time for that lean to carry you off balance, forward, backward or to either side. The higher you are when you jump, more the chance of experiencing that sense of helplessness, and the harder that water would slap you when you met it. And never far from a quarry jumper's mind were the stories of the kids who'd died there, the ones who bounced off the lower rocks, the kid whose neck had snapped on a twig floating in the water. No one could say exactly how big that twig was, or when a twig's size makes it a branch. But we knew he had died.

By the time we got to the last quarry, Kevin had already pulled out. He made no excuses, gave no apologies, and to my surprise no one gave him a hard time. Even Sully had kept his mouth shut. When Kevin quit, saying only, "that's it for me," I just nodded. He was my best friend and we usually knew exactly what the other was thinking. But inside, I couldn't understand why he would stand down without even seeing the jumps of the next quarry. Although he wouldn't make any more high jumps, he continued with us to Tabletop. When he said he was out of it, I'm fairly certain we all felt a sense of envy, and something else too – perhaps respect.

As Sully stepped across the red footsteps, he looked to Ned and snickered. Him, with that crazed laugh, as though he knew something no one else did. His scraggly hair and crooked teeth made him look at home in the surroundings, a natural in the quarry's wildness.

Beyond The Wall was a jump named Ship's Keel. The two sides of the boulders that jutted out there angled toward each other as they reached toward the water, coming to an arrowhead point at the edge.

"It don't matter which one you jump. They're both 50 feet," Ned instructed. "Both, just as dangerous."

But he was wrong.

The Wall was where I would take flight. The idea of following the footprints – the ones someone, for some reason, had taken the time to paint – appealed to me. We walked back to the red marks. The artist had included nice curved arches to his creations. They looked real, the forms like something muddy feet might make on a white surface.

When I looked over the side of The Wall, picturing my path through the air, my chest tightened. The rocks ambling away felt like they were pulling me forward and downward with a force more than gravity. I stepped backward and looked around. Sully's face was stretched a little tight, and his eyes wide, like my own. We'd been watching each other carefully at every jump that day and in the glance from The Wall we shared the realized danger of the place; it was every bit the challenge we'd heard.

"I think I'm with Kevin after this one," Sully finally said. Then he looked toward the edge again. "That's *if* I do it," he added. He looked back toward Ship's Keel a few times. He had not looked up when he spoke, just laid the words out there. I was glad to hear that his fear was about the same as mine, and I knew then I would make this jump.

Not far behind Sully, Ned moved with purpose across Ship's Keel, walking backwards, measuring his steps in the shorter strides that a runner might take. He stared down at the rocks as though seeing his feet hit the same marks on the dash to the edge.

When Ned saw me looking over, he jerked his head up and pumped his left hand in the air, "Yeeaaaaah!" he yelled loudly, as though he felt only the excitement, and none of the fear.

Then Kevin said the words that once would have struck terror in me – "Johnny Ramzee." He said it low, so only I could hear. It had been five years since he'd terrorized us as third-graders.

What the hell is he doing here was my only thought before turning.

"Hey Johnny, what's up?" asked Sully. It was the only time I'd ever heard anyone address Ramzee without fear. It sounded like they were old buddies.

"Just looking at the jumps. You going to do this?" said Ramzee. Then he glanced at me. "Hey, I know you," he said, and squinted like he was trying to remember from where. He was heavier than I'd remembered him. His t-shirt was tight on his fat body and his face was spotted with acne. But mostly, I noted that he wasn't taller than me anymore. I now had an inch over the porcupine kid.

"Yeah, I'm thinking about doing it," I said. "How about you?"

The calmness of my voice surprised me, and the question even held the trace of a challenge. I wasn't sure why, but I was glad for it. I wondered later if it was the height difference or the quarries' unwritten "no-fighting" rule that gave me the boost I needed. In either case, Ramzee looked as surprised as me.

"I don't know," he said, eyeing me. "I might do it after you guys." He glanced quickly at Kevin and Sully, smiled and snapped his head toward the edge. "This is where that kid broke his legs," he said.

At Ship's Keel, Ned yelled. "Sully, come on. Let's go." They were about to search for a boulder to toss off the edge. I figured Sully had somehow signaled Ned that he was heading that way.

"You mean the kid whose father pulled him out?" asked Sully, delaying his trip toward Ned. We had all heard the story of the policeman who pulled his drowning son with two broken legs and a broken arm from the water.

"Yeah, it was right here. They say you got to jump out far to clear the rocks," said Ramzee, glancing from Sully to me. I had stepped backward, but now leaned forward again, propping my left leg at an angle and leaning my bent arm into it as I looked over. Not far from the top, a big rock jutted out about eight feet toward the left, in the angle of the footsteps. It never occurred to me that the jutting rock might be concealing a dangerous bulge in the rock wall further down. I had cleared 13 feet in a long-jump competition a year earlier; I was confidant of clearing that top rock. Yet, I would take no chances. I'd learned at the first quarry to always jump up and out as far as I could: it gave a better sense of control. My main concern was keeping my balance in the air, not tilting forward and smashing face-first into the water.

I was pretty sure Ramzee was just testing me when he mentioned the kid breaking his legs, watching for my reaction. I stood on the last red footprint, looking down, seeing nothing but water beyond and to the sides of the jutting ledge. Then I began stepping backward. The initial shock of hearing Ramzee's name lingered in my chest, even if it hadn't registered in my voice. Already my heart beat fast and I hadn't yet looked for a boulder to toss.

"I'll see you guys in the water," said Ramzee, and then he headed to the other side of The Wall, where he started climbing down the rocks. I stepped back and forth to the edge three times, keeping the steps short. This was when Kevin and I were supposed to find a large rock. Instead, I started backing up again, following the prescribed angle of the footsteps.

Sully and Ned had dropped their boulder near the edge of Ship's Keel and Sully stood to the side waiting for Ned to make his run. The boulder would break the water for Ned: Ned's body would break it for Sully.

With nobody else close enough to hear now, Kevin asked if I was sure I wanted to do the jump. "This is where that kid almost got killed," he added. There were wrinkles in his brow and he was talking low and evenly. "Why don't you do Ship's Keel?"

The fact that he knew what was involved and still objected unnerved me even more. Kevin knew the deal. I could not let Ramzee or Sully see weakness. To back off would be begging for trouble. I expected Kevin would want me to show no fear; instead, he was feeling it for me, with me.

"No way," I said. "I can't back down now," and Kevin didn't say anything more.

The wind was beginning to sound even louder, and I realized how little time was left to find or toss any boulder. The fear was wrestling with me and I didn't know if I could keep it down. *But I should break the water,* I thought. The fear, like vines, climbed up my back, and a voice from deep within spoke urgency. *Now. Now. Now. Don't think about it.* I looked quickly at my feet, then out to the edge of The Wall, and was running.

My right foot made a hard slap on the rock about four inches in from the edge and I sprung well over the jutting rock below. I'd hit my mark with a natural stride, allowing for the good push-off, the toes leaving last. Over the edge and beyond the protruding ledge I began to pull up my knees. *Keep the balance,* I thought.

It was then that I spotted the second jutting rock. At a glance I saw that this one stuck out from a 15-foot bulge in The Wall, just up from the surface. The upper jutting rock had concealed it before, but over the edge I saw it easily. *Shit,* was the initial thought, accompanied by a certainty that I was going to hit it at full speed.

Years later, I can still see that lower rock reaching out, but feel only a shadow of the fear that enveloped me in the air that day. I had followed the blood-red footprints off the edge going at exactly the angle that led to the lower bulge. I know now, it was no coincidence; someone had drawn those prints to lead directly to that hidden ledge.

As I dropped through the air, I moved further from The Wall. Through my legs I saw the rock, still in my glide. It looked like it was square and had somehow turned 45 degrees. Nestled into the hill, its sinister tip jutting outward. Still in the air, I was aware of Ramzee off to my left, on a ledge. For no good reason, it occurred to me that he could already tell whether I'd hit it or not. These were not long thoughts. They were realizations that hit with the speed and impact of lightning. I waited another half second before straightening my back and shooting my legs down. I arched, pulled my fists under my chin, closed my eyes, and waited.

To this day, I wonder what Ramzee was thinking. But frozen in the air above that rock, I thought of nothing at all. Like the air in my lungs, my system stopped. Only when the water surged upward, past my thighs, did I know that the danger had passed. *I made it,* singed through me like the water rushing by.

I held tight to the moment and my position, slicing about 20 feet through the comforting water, then into the freezing sub-surface layer. That ice water hit me like a second power surge to my electrical system. *You can't relax for a second in this place,* I thought. Instinctively, kicking and waving my arms, I stopped my descent and swam upward toward the surface.

My heart beat wildly. Even though my head knew the danger had passed, the heart kept on racing. Breaking the surface of the water, I heard Ramzee.

"I don't believe it! Unbelievable!" He waited till I caught my breath and looked over. "You missed by about this much," he yelled, his hands only inches apart. "Jesus Christ, that was unbelievable," he yelled. I waved my arms slowly in the water to stay afloat and breathed heavily.

"Yeah," I said. "I know," feeling only relief.

Then I was talking, hearing my own words as they came out.

"So are you gonna jump it?"

"What!" Ramzee yelled. "No way in hell!"

If I'd had any energy left, I would have laughed. Instead I only smiled, waving my arms back and forth, floating with a sense of freedom I hadn't felt in awhile, as if I'd stretched the bonds of some invisible force.

CHAPTER XII

THE QUIET TRUTH

I t was near the end of the summer when Ned and I stood on the corner, watching and listening: two young teens on a mission. Ned would take a puff of his cigarette, glance to his left, exhale, take another puff, glance to his right, kick his foot into the ground, say something, exhale and start the routine again. He was more impatient than nervous. It was guilt, fear, and a sense of doom that weighed down on me that twilight evening: it seemed as if some dark magic spell clung to me, and my thinking had been sharpened to only one thought. "It's time."

There was no way back now. There was no chance of avoiding the night's showdown. I had a bad feeling, and my whole future, I felt certain, would proceed well or badly, based on the events of the next hour. Down where I couldn't push it any deeper, I expected the worst.

I could see that Ned viewed it differently. He expected it would go well and I had no idea why. We were facing, I believed, a sure ass kicking; and there he was – all confidence. Normally he was quick with a joke and a laugh and liked to talk, but tonight's venture was a serious one. He wasn't telling me about some crazy character he saw riding the train, or what outrageous statement he heard some bum make. By the curb, he studied the cigarette he held in front of his eyes for a few seconds, close enough to see the circular lines of its paper, and when he tapped it with a quick motion of his pointer finger, the ashes broke free and fell in a single clump down toward the sidewalk. His mouth had the hint of a smile when he glanced back toward me. He was looking forward to the upcoming event – eager, unafraid. My respect for his instincts was carrying me.

It was just after 6 p.m. on the corner of Melbourne Street and Centre Ave. in Dorchester. The two of us stood a half block from Wainwright Park. Over my left shoulder, down Melbourne, on the opposite side of the street, the big kids were already drinking. Their laughter only added to the surreal feelings on the corner. I figured they had enough beer to keep them in place, away from us, for at least another half hour, which I expected to be long enough.

About a football field behind us stood Saint Mark Elementary School. There, the menacing nuns in their black and white garb, with their clickers had nourished their own brand of fear. But tonight's challenge was different: the Wainwright boys didn't play by any of the nuns' rules. They lacked the their discipline, making them immediately more dangerous, though less so in the long run, eternity being what it is.

"How much time you think we got," I asked.

Ned exhaled and glanced again toward the park. "Not long. Five minutes at the most."

I'd better figure out what to say, I thought, surprised I hadn't even considered this yet. After all, I'd known for hours I would have to start the showdown.

The day's drama had begun at four o'clock that afternoon. Then again, it really began at the summer's outset. It was just after we joined the park. Our small group of eight had been sucked into the gang of 27. That was how I saw it then. While I waited I remembered what brought me to Wainwright, and what had happened since then.

To me, Wainwright had always been where the tough boys of Saint Mark Elementary School hung out, and all my memories of it were of violence. It had a reputation as a dangerous place with a rough crew, and I had wanted nothing of them. But all that slipped from my hands. The stories of wild times had convinced the other Lafield boys to make the move. Ned used to hang out there before he linked up with us, so his move back was natural. Kevin had argued that we needed to align ourselves with some larger gang for safety.

The bowling alley, Lucky Strikes, was out of the question; those guys were rats, and none of us were into leather coats and switchblades. Wainwright already included a lot of kids who graduated from Saint Mark, and a few of them had visited with our Lafield Street group before. Never completely convinced that it was the natural progress Kevin made it out to be, I'd been the last to join.

Everyone had been fairly friendly the first week as we checked each other out. But it didn't take long for the meaner spirit to emerge. Sully beating that kid senseless brought the undercurrent right up to the surface. I didn't like the way they picked on each other, either: it was relentless. Just a few weeks before the showdown, there was a name-calling contest. Everybody got ragged on to some extent, and a few of the names stuck. I'd picked up the name "dog;" supposedly because I could run so fast. "Dog;" the name would make me blush with shame.

They treated us worse than their dogs, my mother had said so long ago. I was well aware of the low ranking of dogs, and here I was having that name pinned on me. I didn't like it from the first, and even less when I heard it a week later, and then again. At Mull's house I tried to kill it. There were only six kids in the game room, four of them from the original Lafield group. Flannery said it and laughed while I was at the Ping-Pong table.

Wishing I had a bat in my hand instead of a silly Ping-Pong paddle, I turned on him.

"I don't ever want to hear that name again," I said, flushed red with anger, but already sensing my mistake. Flannery leaned back toward the wall. "It isn't funny, and you've been warned," I added. When he raised his hands as though in surrender, everyone laughed. I wasn't overly strong, and only average height and weight for my age. But I could move quickly and I'd picked up a reputation as a capable fighter from tossing kids around the churchyard in wrestling matches. I didn't like real fights, though: I didn't enjoy the idea of inflicting pain on someone. I liked the idea of receiving it even less.

"When I stomped my foot down on his face. Man!" Paul had recounted to me, once. "It was the *best feeling* I ever had," he said as though I'd understand. "You know?"

I didn't know, and didn't want to. But with the threat at Mull's place, I'd exposed a weakness: I'd announced how anyone could get to me whenever they wanted. With this new crowd, I figured it was just a matter of time before someone would start tapping on that exposed nerve.

At least three of the kids from the park could take me down alone, I knew, but they were not the big threat; that would be the gang rats. Having to take four of five of them on at once – that worried me plenty. I hadn't forgotten Sully's lesson on fairness, or how three of them had ganged up on the kid the night before. It didn't help that I already sensed hostility: whether it was my unwillingness to inflict pain, or something else, didn't matter.

Still waiting on the corner, I remembered the night Sugar Bear, one of the bigger boys, talked about being on the receiving end of a pack attack. He'd coached a group of us.

"Just don't go down," was his advice. "You can take the beatings off the side of the head, the chest, it don't matter; after a while it doesn't even hurt that much. But, if you go down," he said, looking into our eyes to make sure we were listening, "then you're in trouble." He glanced to his side, at his older brother who was about 15 feet away talking to older kids. He lowered his voice, "that's when they start kicking, when they break ribs in your side and bones on your face – you know your nose'll break." He looked over again toward his brother and took a few steps the other way. No one wanted to lose eye contact, and we drifted with him, his voice staying low.

"My brother went down. That's what happened to him," he said. I looked toward his brother, but he was looking the other away. "I kept throwing punches blind and taking the hits," continued Sugar. As he spoke, he raised his arms and swayed smoothly from side to side. "Hold your arms like this," he coached, holding his elbows straight out in front of him, his forearms forming a right angle, fists up over his head, "and keep your head down." He ducked. "Just every now and then throw a punch to keep them from getting too close." He pumped his left arm out a few times. Only when it came back to protect his face did he throw a couple of rights. All the time he swayed, his head ducking down lower sometimes, then coming back up to peek out over his fists. "And keep your back to the wall so they can't get behind you." It sounded like sensible advice to me, not that I expected ever to need it. Not then, anyway.

Behind me was a house with a rock and cement foundation. *OK,* I thought.

Ned finished exhaling, "What are you looking at now?" he asked.

"Nothing."

He glanced again toward the Park.

"Here they come," was all he said. He took another drag on the cigarette and took one step out into the street. I leaned forward and turned left. About five bodies, halfway between the park and the corner, walked through the twilight toward us.

"Hobano," yelled Flannery with a confident sound. He was playing off Ned's last name, Hobin. "What are you doing here?" They were all park regulars, none of the Lafield boys: five against two, I thought as I felt my chest rise, and hoped my voice would hold.

It was that afternoon when Ned had banged on my door. I answered, surprised. We had always met at the corner; he'd never been to my door before. His face was red, like he had been running, and his eyes wide open, excited. I figured he was in some kind of trouble.

He told me he had something I needed to hear, and he held something up that was wrapped in paper.

"It's a record," he said, his wide eyes and expression telling me there was more. "You are going to want to hear this," he added, waving the covered, vinyl 45-rpm disk. "Let's go to my house, though. I'll tell you about it on the way."

On the way, I learned that Ned, Flannery, and a few more of the park regulars had thumbed the 20 miles to Nantasket Beach that day. Across from the beach, they visited Paragon Park and some record-making booth.

"You need to hear what they had to say," said Ned.

I tried to hide the sinking feeling in my gut. Ned, on the other hand was growing more animated.

"You know, these guys were just pissing me off. They never say anything to your face, but man, once they get behind your back," he said, and then just looked me in the eyes and shook his head. "Well, I got it all right here. That name you don't like." He knew me well enough to not say it. "It's here," he finished, watching me, apparently for some sign of rage.

My heart was in my shoes and I looked at Ned wondering if he really thought he was doing me a favor. He knew those guys. I had been hoping that the name would go away. I hadn't heard it for the past few weeks, since Mull's house, but now Ned had the evidence.

"Do you really think I want to hear that?" I asked.

Ned was dumbfounded. "Of course you do," he said, after a second. "They're only going to deny it. But they were shooting their mouths off while the record was playing. You need to hear it," he said, looking as though my question had confused him. Then his eyes took on a sharper focus.

"And you need to do something about it too," he said.

At first, I wasn't sure, then realized he knew exactly what he was saying.

"And what are you going to do?" I snapped back, hot with shame and anger.

"I'll go with you," he said. "If you need help, I'm with you."

Up in his room, Ned and I listened to the evidence. The three-minute recording was rough, as though the microphone was being waved around the air from a short distance. There was some singing, some swearing, some name-calling and my new nickname mentioned a few times, once loud in the clear voice of Flannery. It was about six o'clock that night when Ned came by to pick me up, and we headed to the park together.

In between, I had thought plenty, and realized that there was no way out. That name bore into me deeper than I could ever explain, and I had no idea how to squash it. I'd never seen anyone forcibly shake a street name before. I would go to the park with Ned and the two of us, outnumbered, were going to get our asses solidly kicked. Only that much seemed clear.

But, Ned was something else. He was tight with these guys. Why was he willing to blow the whistle on them like he did, I wondered. And he was willing to take the beating with me. I searched for some reason, but could find no sense in it. He and I liked each other, but we weren't best friends. The more I thought about it, the more Ned stood only to lose because of his actions: it was a no-gainer. When I asked him why, back at his house, his answer had awoken something up in me.

"I just didn't like the way they were treating you," he explained, as though it should have been obvious. "There was no reason for it." It was that simple to him. I looked at him, thinking, there had to be more. "It just wasn't right," was all he added.

Here was someone who wasn't out for just himself. He was willing to make himself a permanent target for future harassment, just because it didn't seem right. His reason came from a place I'd forgotten; a clean, uncluttered place. The offer to assist came with no talk of allegiances, past favors, future promises, and it wasn't even being done for me.

Ned had not responded to the "Hobano" call.

I took another step forward by the street light in time to see a short one – got to be Sully, I figured – skip forward and punch Flannery on the arm while jerking his head in my direction.

"Healy! What are you doing here?" said Flannery in a snickering manner, as though sharing a joke with his crew.

"To see you, loudmouth," I answered. I never had figured out what to say, but Flannery's attitude was making it easy.

"What?" said Flannery. His smile shifted, leaving a confused slant to his mouth.

"I said I'm here to see you."

"Me, why? What for?" Then, he looked toward Ned, put the pieces together, and back to me.

The group had spread out now, the others glancing at each other, trying to get a consensus of whether this was just between me and Flannery, or all of them against Ned and me.

I stepped into the street.

"Come on over," I said, my voice holding up. "Let's talk about what you did today, and," I hesitated just a second, "what you said." He was quiet now, just looking, mind racing.

"I listened to a record earlier."

At the time, I had no idea of how to proceed. I had never before deliberately provoked a fight. The few I'd been in had all happened spontaneously; there was a push, an elbow, someone swung, and there was a fight – they basically self-started. This was different. I knew there had to be some procedure here, but I didn't know it. I felt awkward – *not good!* – I wanted to get to the action quickly, but didn't know how.

"Sure, I'll come over," Flannery finally said. With this he took three steps away from the comfort of his crowd. None of them were interjecting themselves into the conversation. It was then when I sensed that none of them really minded the idea of seeing Flannery take a beating. I had little fear of him. At that time, he was a pale-faced skinny kid with little athletic ability, mostly someone who talked a lot.

His walk was slow and he strayed: he was scared.

"What, you're going to kick my ass? So what, what's that going to prove?"

"It's not going to prove anything. You heard what I said before."

I knew he was stalling, but felt stuck in this dance where I didn't know the steps.

"You didn't like what I said on the record. So what, you're going to beat me up?" The pitch in his voice had gone up a notch and he was talking too quickly. When his eyes stopped moving around, he looked straight at me. "But, I wasn't the only one on that record," he said. Then, not only his eyes, his whole face seemed to open up, like he had spotted something from me. "And maybe you can't beat up someone else who was on it so easy."

"What are you talking about?"

"I ain't going to say, but you know. Someone else, someone maybe you can't beat up, was on that record too."

I looked back at the crowd. They looked from Flannery to each other, only Sully meeting my eyes with his usual crooked smile, like he knew exactly where this was going, and was enjoying it. I heard myself talking.

"Yours is the only voice I heard."

"What! Come on, you know who. How'd you find out about this anyway, Ned? He knows who else was saying it, why don't you ask him?"

With this Ned, pulled the cigarette from his mouth, holding his hands off to the side in a wide gesture of amazement.

"Don't listen to his shit. Kick his ass!"

I wanted to, but the problem was, Flannery was right.

"You know you're a pretty worthless piece of shit," I said. "A coward."

But the words had no effect. It was a dodge, as much as Flannery's delaying tactics; I was fooling no one, especially, not myself.

He only looked back at me, not needing to say a word. So, I turned to Mulaney.

"I guess he's talking about you."

The time for the group to take us on, by then, had passed. The glances in the early part of the confrontation had ended without action. Now, one of the group had turned on another. Flannery hadn't called him by name, but he had definitely steered me to Mulaney. A bigger, more dangerous enemy, Mulaney had some athletic ability and a bulky body. I'd never seen him fight, but I'd never seen anyone challenge him, either.

"I ain't going to fight you," said Mulaney.

I tried to hold on to my anger and not show the relief.

"What are you saying? You're afraid?"

He shook his head side to side, not looking at me, but watching from the corner of his eye.

"I just ain't going to fight," he said. I was truly surprised.

"This is the big, bad park boys? And you ain't going to fight?" Flannery had been right. I didn't think I could beat Mulaney. I never even considered that he might back down.

I stepped toward him, and he stepped back, pulling something from his pocket.

"What's that," I asked.

"I ain't going to fight you. I'd use a knife if I had one, but all I got is this screwdriver, and I'll use it if I have to."

I've won already, I thought. But, it had gone too easy; I figured somehow pain had to get involved.

"You're a piece of shit too," I offered. He said nothing. "These are your friends you're standing in front of. You're about four inches taller than me, about 30 pounds heavier, and you won't fight me without a screwdriver?" I was beginning to absorb Ned's confidence, as he stood off to the side, just watching.

The screwdriver's metal caught the streetlight. The base was about three inches of transparent, thick yellow plastic. From it, jutted out four inches of metal. Mulaney put the base into the heel of his right hand and folded his fingers over the top of it, the metal portion jutting out from between the middle of his fingers. That grip makes no sense, I thought, and wondered if he was just now trying to figure out how he'd use it. *Didn't he think of that before he put it in his pocket?*

"I wouldn't back down in front of anybody," I continued. "I suppose I could call your mother every name in the book." He said nothing. He was still handling the screwdriver, the thumb and two fingers of his left hand touching the protruding metal. I felt muscles in my upper back tighten instinctively, as though my body understood a threat my mind hadn't.

"OK, she's a dirt bag too, probably a slut to have a dirt bag like you."

"It don't matter what you say, I ain't fighting," he said, neither moving farther away, nor stepping closer. It wasn't until later that I realized how quickly he could have changed the grip on the screwdriver. His friends started shifting their feet, but said nothing to urge him on, either.

"What about you," I asked Flannery, turning to him, guessing that I should be the one talking.

"I'm not fighting either," he answered.

"I knew it," said Ned. It was just the push I needed.

"These are your friends," I said to the other three. "Take a good look. They're just a couple of cowards. Would any of you back down like this?" I wasn't sure about any of them, other than Sully. We'd be halfway through this thing if it was he was out front. What I had dreaded was getting jumped or hounded by this group in front of me. I realized now, I was way off base. The only glue to them was the fear and intimidation they practiced on each other. By nightfall, all of the park would know of their cowardice; their friends would make sure of it.

"Last chance," I said. "Are either of you going to fight, or just let everyone know what cowards you are?"

"I ain't fighting you," said Mulaney.

"No," said Flannery.

I knew then I'd never hear that street name again; it would only serve as a reminder of their shame. I looked over toward Ned, and he made no sign either way, looking instead toward the group. There was only silence for a short while, till Sully spoke up.

"So, you guys going to the park?" he asked, looking toward Ned.

"What do you say?" said Ned, looking to me.

"No thanks."

"Me either," said Ned.

The boys, murmuring among themselves, turned back toward the park they had left. Ned and I watched for a few seconds and then headed the other way, back toward the old schoolyard. I was already committing the action and exact words to memory, and it was playing well. *I'd stepped forward, he'd stepped back. I'd called him a dirt bag, a coward.* Three steps down the road, the parts that gnawed at me were quickly fading. It was then that the silence from Ned rolled over me. My mind got quiet for a second or two, until a question eased in. *Why isn't he congratulating me?* It's funny how sometimes you see a kid and feel like you know him better than he'll ever know himself. There's things he doesn't want to know, so he doesn't. I suddenly felt on the wrong side of that situation.

In the quiet, I felt it sink in: I'd been kidding myself. I'd buried parts of the night already, and I didn't even know how many. I figured Ned knew just about everything about me as we walked in silence toward the old school. For reasons better than mine, he'd taken the same risk; and more importantly, he wasn't burying anything. His view became more than just important, and I wondered what it was he knew.

He knew I had been afraid of facing the gang. He knew I had been afraid of facing Mulaney. It was possible that without his pushing, I might never have even gone looking for anyone that night. He knew that, too. *Did he think I'd done enough?* Ten steps along now, and the silence still floated. When I glanced over at him, he was staring straight ahead, eyes slightly unfocused; no clue to what that mind held.

If it were him, the fight would have happened. I knew too, I could have forced the fight with Mulaney. "I suppose I could call your mother . . ." How weak was that? Still staring straight ahead, Ned lit a cigarette, and handed the matches and the pack over to me. Only then did he speak.

"You did OK back there, G-Man," he said. It was a name he used when he was in a good mood, playing off my true name, Gerard. He accused me of nothing, though he knew exactly where my mind was. "But you should have kicked their asses."

I didn't say anything. I had no heart to bullshit him, or intention to deny my cowardice.

"Especially Flannery," he continued. "He was scared shit," his tone had become playful now, his voice rising, and I was beginning to feel better. "Why are you picking on me?" he mimicked in a wimpy voice. "Why don't you pick on someone else?" Then he started laughing. It was a beautiful, loud laugh, sending a message halfway back to the park where I knew they could hear it. For a second that worried me, and then a smile rippled across my face. We kept walking as a dark heaviness floated from my shoulders up into the cooling night air. *It was going to be all right, after all.*

Ned wouldn't let it go there, though. He looked over with a mock face of shocked horror, his mouth opened wide and his eyes bulging. This time he was outright yelling. "Why are you picking on me!" he boomed, following with a laugh that covered the entire neighborhood. It was, I realized even then, a moment.

Those eyes have lost none of their spark; that skin has never wrinkled; and the melody of that wild laugh is just as sweet. As much as anything I did that night, that rippling sound broke forever the dark spell of the gang. Standing up to them, it seemed, had been enough. We continued down the avenue, just past the elementary school before turning up Centre Street. By then, I'd relaxed enough to laugh too; a softer laugh that came out in erratic jerks, like something escaping. I don't remember where we went afterward, or either of us saying anything else. In my mind, the night ended there, with only laughter filling the air.

CHAPTER XIII

GENTLE FALL

The summer passed quickly after we walked away from the park, and fall, with all its color, arrived. One October day in particular that year still resonates brightly in my mind. The sun was brilliant, illuminating the whole town that Saturday afternoon, and blinding anyone who would look straight into it. Beneath it, all of Dorchester including Stevie and me, watched the yellow, red, and wild orange leaves fly about. Plenty was happening in the rest of the world, but up on the garage roof, all was quiet. In the distance you could hear the voices of little kids. They were yelling, two or three neighborhoods away, as though celebrating not just that day, but the whole season of change. As the summer had ended that year I felt like I'd escaped from prison, a prison whose bars were of my own making. But now there were new things on the horizon, I just wasn't sure yet what they might be.

Looking south from the gentle, sloping angle of Smith's garage, my 14-year-old eyes gazed at the widening trees to the larger houses of

King Street. Folks with money lived there. Unlike the houses of Lafield, those houses were wider with bulges along some sides boasting of the round rooms within. I figured 20, 30 years ago, these were the mansions where servants carried food and drinks on trays to the owners. Going to the right on King Street took you to the side lawn of the Saint Mark Catholic Church. It had been years since I'd walked across that lawn in that First Holy Communion procession, dressed in white shirt, white tie, white pants, and little white suit coat. Beyond the church was the convent of the Sisters of Notre Dame.

King Street was just two blocks from Lafield, but man, it was a whole other world. That's where kids carried their books in new, brightly colored bags, and you knew their white Lent boxes would be full to the brim when the time came. The nuns would shake those coins around, smiling at the King Street kids. Those of us with the half-empty boxes got only nods of acknowledgement.

My mind wandered as Stevie talked in the background. At 16, he was one of the older kids, so when he asked me to hang out with him, I didn't argue. It was strange that he would be hanging out with someone two years his junior. Not the type to share beer for no reason, I figured he was up to something.

Somewhere out of sight, a bird was singing high notes in different patterns. After a brief pause, it stopped, and then started again with a different routine. From the background, some of Stevie's words broke through. "Three girls, all sisters," was the phrase. This was something I knew little about – girls. Not since one beautiful, blond-haired Meredith DeVoe had broken my heart.

"What girls are they?" I asked, in as uninterested a manner as I could. Stevie looked down toward his beer can, stalling. He was about three inches taller than me, with an uneven bony head – wide in the back, narrowing toward the front, where it ran into an almost board-straight forehead. From the middle of his face came an angular, sharp nose. He was delaying way too long, playing me I knew, but made like I didn't.

"The girls?" he tossed back.

"Yeah." I pulled the cold can of Schlitz up for a swig.

"They're the ones that live up by King's Market on the other end of King Street, right on the top of the hill." Steve stretched out his arm, holding the beer can with the bottom three fingers and thumb of his left hand, index finger pointing in the opposite direction of the convent.

I turned my head to the left, but all I was seeing was Meredith, with her blond curls, sparkling blue eyes, and polite manner. And with a name like DeVoe, I – and the whole seventh grade at the time – knew she was destined for stardom.

Without saying a word she'd crushed me. We'd walked to a drugstore and she let me buy her a coke. We shared it as we made our way back to her house. Grandma – there was no mother or father around – was walking back and forth slowly on the front porch as we came closer. It was a hot day, but there she was with that shawl around her, and her gray and black strands of hair pulled tight behind a wrinkled face. Later, I wondered, if she spoke only German, or if there was some other reason why I rated only a short nod of the head. Meredith had looked up at her quickly before sliding through the door, and grandma had stayed, watching from the porch until I was clear off the street.

"So, how old are they?" I asked.

"Well, like I said, there are three of them," answered Stevie, warming to the topic. "I think the youngest is like 12, then 14 and 16." He took another sip, "You know," he said in the manner of a coach advising a rookie, "I'll bet the 12-year-old is going to be the best looking of them all."

I wondered what Stevie would consider good looking, and said, "OK, you can have the 12-year-old."

"I didn't say that," Steve snapped, voice rising. "Don't get smart."

I smiled, but I didn't miss the warning. I had to be careful with Steve, he was someone who could go off the deep end and I'd be in trouble.

I wasn't sure what had gone wrong with Meredith. I'd had a good time; I thought she did too. It was a week later when Debbie Lesley delivered the bad news. "I'm sorry to hear about you and Meredith," was how she hit me with it.

What, what about us? I'd wondered. I never had to say the actual words.

"Oh, I thought you heard," she said and hesitated; looking worried by my confused expression. "I mean. I heard she thought you were *nice*. She really did. She thought you were . . . OK. Just, she was more interested in, you know – Mark."

The noise of the kids brought me back, it sounded like they were playing street football. I brought the Schlitz can up to my mouth and just as I tilted it upward, Steve finally got to it.

"So do you want to visit them?"

All visions of Meredith and whatever Mark might have looked like deserted me. I looked around, the roof suddenly seeming smaller.

"You said the young girl was the best looking. How about the others? How about the 14-year-old? How's she look?" I asked.

"She's all right. I think she's your type even, not bad looking at all," said Stevie. "So, how about it, want to visit them?"

I tried, without luck, to picture exactly, my type; it wouldn't be Meredith that was for sure. I liked the "not-bad looking" part, but I figured that was just bait for the trap. I could sense the garage roof dropping from beneath my sorry butt. The girls were probably as ugly as hell, except for maybe the oldest one, who would not be interested in a 14-year-old. But to back out now would leave me looking like I was afraid of girls; and this being true, I really had no choice. Stevie was slippery all right: he'd set it up nice.

"Sure," I said. "But let's finish the beer first."

I listened jealously to the kids yelling in the distance: it sounded as if they were really getting into the game. I felt the fleeting sensation of confidence, picturing a long touchdown pass. I was reaching for it when a sharp wind brought me back.

Off the roof, over Smith's fence, across a back yard and out onto King Street, Stevie and I headed up the hill. It was one of those times where you want the day to stand still, the sun getting warmer, the promise of adventure, and a meeting with girls on the horizon. I was enjoying the walk, the lingering buzz, and the promise of that sunny afternoon. But my limited experience with girls told me that the anticipation would likely be the day's highlight. As we made our way up the hill, I wondered why that was. What was it with girls? It's true, I had two rather over-sized front teeth and a bit of a pale complexion, and who knew plaid shorts didn't mix with striped shirts? Girls, that's who. Where did they learn these rules anyway? They did a whole lot of looking and not too much talking, at least not to the guys, not to me. They'd stand about in mini-circles, speaking inward, occasionally glancing out. They were just too much, and I had my hands full already dealing with characters like Stevie. Is that why I got the beers, because of my teeth? He usually wasn't much for talking, Stevie: like he was afraid to let you know what he was thinking. But today was different; the more he thought about those girls, the more he talked.

"OK, we'll just say we were going to the store when we see them, right? The market is right across the street from their house. If they're not there, we can even get a couple of cokes and hang around drinking them till they show up." It was all Mission Impossible.

Without looking I could sense him watching for my reaction. The real question still, "was I in, or was I out?" If out, Steve knew that I'd hang around about five minutes or so, then take off, leaving him to face the trio alone. Not even God could help him then, I figured.

"So, that's the plan, huh?" I said. He waited while I kicked a bottle cap out into the street. It jumped high and skipped away. "Sure, sounds good to me," I answered. "I got enough for a coke." I could sense his relief.

"This is going to be all right," he said. He had a smile on his face, like he actually had a good feeling.

I'd come across him years ago when he was shaking down a younger kid for his money. He'd backed him out on to the large rocks of Malibu Beach, told him he was going to drown him first, then take not only his change, but his bathing suit too. Terrified, the kid had given up the 85 cents.

We made our way up King Street to where it intersected with Adams. The traffic was light, but the few drivers on Adams were in a hurry, as usual. A southbound bus broke the rhythm, wheezing by like an old dog. Across the street on the left was the Hemenway schoolyard and beyond that, the Hemenway Public School – an overbearing, dark brick, five-story building.

Beyond the Hemenway, at the top of the King Street's hill sat a two-story wooden house, something out of Hansel and Gretel. There was the fence, the kind you could hop over with just one arm, not high. Then the row of cement squares on the other side, leading up to the steps. Between the cement squares was grass, not cut close, but not as wild as I would have liked. Before the stairs, on the left was a huge tree, spreading its branches wide, fending off the burning rays of the sun. Beneath that protection sat two girls on the bottom stairs and the 16-year-old a few steps higher. They were the welcoming touches of a promising day, three curious-eyed girls. I could hear that unique slang in their voices before they even said *hey*.

All I saw of the house and the residents was caught in a quick glance to the right, long enough to catch my breath and feel the day's heat in a rush.

"Hey," said Steve, a second later. A slow look back and I saw the girl on the fourth stair hesitate, and then she gave a quick wave. "Hey!" We were still walking, past the house, out onto the street, and then into the King Street Market. I turned to Stevie.

"Hey?" I said. "That's it, Hey?"

"You said you wanted a coke, right?"

"What?"

"A coke, right? You said you wanted a coke, didn't you."

I thought Steve had actually gone insane. "No. I didn't. I said I could *afford* a coke." Did he forget about the girls and remember only the coke?

The guy behind the counter yelled over, asking if he could help us.

Stevie had already grabbed two cokes from the side counter. "Here, this is it," he said, holding up the bottles. I dropped my change on the counter, and, using the opener by the door, popped off the bottle cap before heading out.

Across the street, the youngest of the girls leaned on the gate. She looked over as though there was nothing better to do on this long, dull day. The game was about to begin, and she was sizing up the competition. I was surprised that it was the young one who had come forward, while the others talked low to each other on the steps. They glanced over a couple of times, never together, first one, then the other.

When Steve came out, we stepped into the shade next to the store and started drinking the cokes. He waited for the 16-year-old to look.

"Hey," he said, while waving. I looked over, but he ignored it.

"Let's go," he said lowly, and we crossed the street.

"I know you," the oldest girl called to Steve. "You're in one of my classes."

"That's right. You don't remember which one?"

The other girl on the stairs leaned over and turned on a transistor radio, and the song burst out. A gaggle of instruments stretched out a melody. Trying to catch them, a persistent voice with a sense of nostalgia crooned.

She raised her face slowly, smiling. Her light brown hair fell from smooth shoulders as she looked up. Tanned skin shined in the sun and her eyes were huge, burning right into mine. Then she laughed.

"What's with you?" she asked, eyes sparkling. "What are you smiling at?"

"I don't know," I said, watching those eyes. "I didn't know I was. Just like the song, I guess."

"Yeah, I guess," she said. Little sister looked back over her right shoulder and they shared a smile.

Stevie and big sister seemed to be getting along all right, and after a few minutes, he talked us into the yard and onto the stairs.

After that, Mary, the one with the radio, admitted she liked the song too. We even mumbled a few bars together. When big sister suggested we all take a walk, no one argued. Elmdale Street angled down the hill till it ran into Adams. Twenty feet to the right was an old complex known as the projects. A ledge of old railroad ties guarded one side of the brick building. We sat on the ties struggling for something to talk about.

Steve and his girl sat to our left. About eight feet from them sat Mary, and I was on her other side, close, but not quite touching. Little sister walked about, stopping every now and then to kick a stone, and stealing off-and-on glances at the four of us.

"How come you stopped singing that song?" Mary asked.

"I don't know. I just stopped, tired of singing, probably."

"No, I don't think so. You stopped all of a sudden like."

"Yeah," I said. It was all I could think to say. Then I turned my head toward Stevie. I was expecting Mary to make a crack about my voice, but she didn't say a word. Stevie had slid closer toward the street, and Big sister had stepped in behind the logs, rubbing his back. "Yeah, that's it. Right there," said Stevie.

"Yeah, I really like that song, too," Mary said finally. She looked like she was thinking about something else, and then she followed my eyes to Stevie and her sister. "Do you like that?" she asked, her voice softer, quieter than before.

I wasn't sure if she was still talking about the song or what we just looked at, but I nodded my head anyway. On the ground, our shadows were closer together. When she would look toward me, her nose and mouth were just inches from the side of my head. "I think so," I said.

"You want *me* to give *you* a massage?" she asked. Her voice had a smooth sound to it, almost like music. The words didn't matter; the voice was saying something all by itself. It was taking me somewhere, somewhere nice.

"Sure."

She stepped over the railroad ties, shifted behind me and placed both lower palms on the top of my neck, then, she slid them down, dragging the back of my t-shirt with the heels of her hand. She laughed as the front of my t-shirt rose up to my Adam's apple. Then she pulled back her hands, dropped them, and brought them back up under the shirt. Leaning forward, with her warm palms she found the skinny tense tendons that ran from my neck to my shoulders. You couldn't tell whose shadow was whose now.

It's like the music, no, it's like color, I thought. You can look at a row of bikes. One can have the same height, same shining white metal, and ride just as smooth as the one beside it. But somehow, the red one is different: it's better. The color tells you something, something you don't really understand, you only feel. That's how her voice was, like a song reaching right into me.

"You nervous or something," she asked. "Your back is all tight." The sound was still smooth, but slightly different. I figured she was smiling. Little sister glanced over, a studious look on her face.

I wondered if she liked me. Mary, that is. When I turned to look at her, the hands loosened. My head swung back without missing a beat.

"Did you ever hear of Specks O'Keefe?" I asked. The hands moved farther down my back. It wasn't just the heat; her hands were strong. I wondered if it could feel even better if my back was actually sore.

"Huh?"

"Specks O'Keefe," I repeated. "He was one of the Brinks Robbery guys."

Stevie had said something to the sister and she giggled loudly, the way people do when they don't really think something's funny.

"He got shot in there," I said, pointing past the shadows, toward the projects. She took her hands from under my shirt and squeezed just inside my shoulders. "Your muscles really are tight," she said. *She said muscles.*

"They're strong. Do you play basketball?"

"Sometimes. I used to play a lot more."

Little sister was back to focusing on a rock as it skipped across the ground. I noticed how she wasn't looking at us, now and I wondered if I was missing something, and if she might tell me later.

"It was in the 50s," I said. "They say he got shot through a window. Later he walked all the way to Codman Square where a friend of his took the bullet out." It was a true story and not many people knew it. It was the best I had.

Using just three fingers of each hand she began to massage each side of my neck, working her way up to my hair. Little sister was kicking the same stone now, as though she'd found just the right one. It would skip across the tar about 10 feet and bounce into a railroad tie. If it bounced up high, she'd try to catch it on the top of her sneaker. I saw that she was pretty good and I wondered how many times she'd been here.

It seemed like forever, but it was probably only ten or so minutes when big sister spoke. "Hey, you guys need to cool down over there."

"What are you talking about," said Mary. "We're not doing anything."

We're not, I thought? She was, by the way, rubbing my neck. And we had been talking, weren't we? Why didn't she say that? How can you not be doing anything? I mean, it was something.

Big sister had stopped working on Stevie and was back in front of him. He was looking downward, arms propped out at sharp angles toward the top tie. She was facing him, talking low, like she was telling him something he didn't want to hear.

Mary took her hands from my neck and gave about six quick karate chops from one shoulder blade to the other.

"That loosens you up," she said. Then, from outside my t-shirt, she grabbed my back and pushed the heels of her hands into it.

"Did he die," she asked.

"Who?"

"The guy who got shot," little sister yelled back, eyes all over her stone as it arched in the air. Mary rested one hand inside my right shoulder. It was warm. "Yeah, him," she said. Little sister caught the rock with her right sneaker and balanced it there for a few seconds.

"No. This all happened before he got caught for the bank robbery," I said. "He lived to rob another day."

"OK, girls. Let's go," big sister said suddenly.

"Now?" said Mary, a wonderful note of disappointment in her voice.

Big sister looked back at her, hands on her hips, and nodded her head.

Little sis flipped a rock up with her toes a few inches, when it started to come back down; she gave it quick kick, and then caught it in her right hand. She looked over toward us with obvious pride. "I wonder what's for dinner?"

Over my shoulder, Mary leaned in. "It was really nice talking to you," she said, sounding just a little sad. I was thinking about a good response when she added, "I had a good time."

All right, I thought. "Maybe I'll see you again."

"I'd like to," she hesitated. "But I can't." That was when time stopped. The voice sounded like it was telling me the opposite of her words. "I got a boyfriend already."

Her face was only inches from my half-turned head, her eyes too close for me to focus on. Her hand still rested warm on my back, her hair brushing my shoulder.

"I know," she said, stepping back. "I shouldn't have even come down here with you. But, he's at the movies today with some guys, so . . ." and she shrugged her shoulders.

Down her back fell the whole world: North America, South America, Australia, Africa, all of it – me too –splashing down into the oceans. And she hardly noticed.

"Anyway, I did like being with you," she offered. "I can tell you're really *a nice guy.* You're not mad are you?"

"No."

"I liked the story about the bank robber too," she said. "Is it true? It really happened here?"

"Yeah."

She squeezed my shoulders. Her fingers tightened, loosened, then began to tighten again before she let go to turn and walk away. Both sisters were waiting for her and the three of them started up the street. I watched for a few seconds before I yelled, "Hey." She turned as though she'd been waiting for it. Her lips were closed and eyebrows up, as though she thought I might be mad.

"Thanks for the massage."

Her lips parted, then she raised her hands up as though someone was robbing her, curled her fingers forward, squeezing the air. Her mouth took on a widening smile. "My pleasure," she said in a soft, rich tone. When she laughed, little sister pushed her, and the two of them ran up the street.

Stevie shook his head. "What's with her?" he asked. We dodged the traffic of Adams, before turning up Centre Street.

"You know Stevie, you were right," I said. "That was a good time."

"It was all right." He said, looking over, "it could have been better." He kept looking to see if I knew what he was talking about.

I knew he'd wanted something more, something big sister wouldn't give. Maybe she could see inside him too. I remembered how he'd taken the money at Malibu that day, and how his victim asked me not to tell anyone. If he didn't get something, especially something he had no right to, Stevie felt like he lost.

"I don't know," I said. "I thought it was real good."

In the distance I could still hear little kids, their yells and screams had a singsong melody. But I didn't feel anything like I did when I'd heard them before. I pictured a young body stretched out reaching for a pass, just steps from the curb. I thought that kid would be watching the spin of the ball close, his stride would have adjusted to its path, he'd have positioned his body at that slight angle – the one that would keep the defender off him and give his arms and hands a little maneuver room. He'd pull the ball in and hop up over the curb in stride. I was happy for him, but not jealous like before. There was something nice in that fall air, something fresh, something new.

Stevie and I headed back up the same road Specks had taken long ago. I thought about how he had made it all the way to Codman Square, losing blood every step of the way. Is that why she held her hands up, I wondered? I figured I'd have made it to the square too, just a matter of hanging on, one step at a time.

"My pleasure," she'd said, and the wind picked up, sending wild red and orange leaves dancing through the air.

EPILOGUE

THE RECEPTION

It was 1998, 31 years since that summer of '67, the year I'd survived The Wall, and with a good friend's help, broke free of the park's mysterious hold. Life had moved along – high school, track, football, girls, college, the military, and marriage had all occurred in the years between.

I spent a day walking around Dorchester's familiar streets. Lafield was as welcoming as always. Number 10 still looked good, no peeling paint, no unkempt hedges. I was glad for it, and tempted to knock on the door to thank the current occupant.

Up Centre Street, the houses appeared neater than I'd remembered them. Passing Dave's house, I glanced up to the third floor and wondered if those who lived there knew what had happened, how his body was found hanging there in the bedroom closet. The death, ruled a suicide, occurred only a few years after we'd watched the rat's miracle escape.

Farther up the road, I saw that Saint Mark's Elementary School had closed its hallways, no longer patrolled by the ladies in black. The faded brick building behind iron gates looked in a state of penance.

Continuing up Centre Ave., bittersweet nostalgia turned cool. The dreary people I passed looked pre-occupied, hurrying along their way. The houses seemed smaller, weeds clogged the entrance to the Tranie, and the long stretch of pebbled surface appeared long abandoned.

At the corner of Melbourne I tried to resurrect that night I had revisited so often over the years. I tried to picture Ned and I against the five, but it was different now. The image that came was only of little kids squabbling on a corner, one of them more afraid than I wanted to remember.

It had been years since Mike Columbo had passed away. Sully, I heard, was in a mental institution; one that Joey Mull had spent time in, as well.

The next day, I attended Ned and Laura's wedding and reception. Halfway through his fireman's career, Ned had decided to settle down at last. Kevin had taken a break from teaching kids with special education needs in Maine to come down for the wedding. A major in the Army, I'd come up from Fort McPherson, Georgia.

Around us, groups of firemen and clusters of some of the Wainwright Park boys were loud in conversations. At out own table, we started trading old stories of the Lafield days, and the laughter came alive. "Anybody up for a game of halfball after this?" Mike joked.

It was like the flash of a camera. For a second or two, there we all were, back on the corner, each watching someone swinging a broomstick at a fluttering half-ball. No doubt we all saw it from our own angles, but from the smiles it was clear the feeling was the same. For the moment, the world existed again only for our enjoyment, our only job to find the adventure; together, capture the excitement. And what in the whole world on a bright summer day could be better than smacking a halfball over a three-decker roof? The melody and rhythms of the laughs were familiar, unchanged by the years

"Those were good times," said Kevin. "Yeah," a few responded, while others nodded, and for a few seconds more we shared the feeling, no one wanting to break the spell.

Back Row: Tom, Mike, Murph, Ned, Kevin, Billy
Front Row: Stevie, Jimmy, Jerry

CPSIA information can be obtained at www.ICGtesting.com
Printed in the USA
BVOW07s0922141014

370660BV00001B/71/P